Psalm 23

A Journey Through the Pasture

A story-led exploration of scriptural truths
about the Good Shepherd's Care

Terry Anderson

ANT Farm Books

Denver, Colorado

Dedication

If I were to name every person who contributed to the person I am today, the dedication would be longer than the book. I dedicate this to the many hands that held me, the voices that guided me, and the hearts that prayed for me. I am deeply indebted to those who have shaped my journey as a follower of Christ. The mentors who modeled His grace and the family and friends who sharpened my spirit. To my community, both near and far: thank you for being in my corner and cheering me on in my peaks and valleys. I am especially humbled by the prayers you whispered on my behalf in the quiet hours, carrying me when I didn't even know I was being held. This book is a harvest from the seeds you all planted.

Table of Contents

Introduction

Psalm 23 has comforted hearts and renewed spirits of believers for generations. Its words are frequently read in moments of peace and in times of pain. Often at the beginning of life and near its end. Yet no matter how familiar the Psalm may become, it always invites us to look closer, to linger a little longer, and to rediscover what it means to truly be cared for and live in fellowship with the Good Shepherd. This book was written to help readers do just that, to slow down and venture through Psalm 23 verse by verse, thought by thought, moment by moment. It will take readers on a journey through that familiar pasture, not just to study its words, but to experience the Shepherd's presence in them. This book will explore each section of the psalm and pair it with real-life reflections, biblical insights, and a personal story that bring the scriptures to life. It is an opportunity to step into our personal pastures and reflect on how the Good Shepherd's care reaches into every portion of our lives.

Think of this book as a companion for reflection. It does not need to be read all at once. The reader can take it part by part, allowing for internal processing and reflection on each section. The reader is invited to sit and rest with the imagery of green pastures, still waters, and overflowing cups. Letting the words stir and recount memories from throughout their own lives.

The purpose of this book isn't to analyze or theologize every scripture, but to encounter the Psalm not as a lesson but as an experience. Psalm 23 is not a distant poem about God's charm; it is a lived testimony of His character and presence. David did not write these words as theory or allegory, but from personal experience and expertise. A shepherd that led flocks, walked through valleys, prepared pastures, and fought off enemies for his flock; speaking to how we can live under the ultimate shepherd's care today.

My hope is that each reader goes on a journey, and within the words of these passages they find courage in the valleys and recognize the overflowing goodness that follows us daily. I pray, that as readers venture thought these pages, they will find their own story within these words, and that this voyage may help each reader find rest, renewal, and assurance in the care of the Good Shepherd who promises that we will dwell in His house now and forever.

PART I

Psalm 23 (NIV)

[1] **The Lord is my shepherd**, I lack nothing.

[2] He makes me lie down in green pastures, he leads me beside quiet waters,

[3] he refreshes my soul. He guides me along the right paths for his name's sake.

[4] Even though I walk through the darkest valley, I will fear no evil, for you are with me; your rod and your staff, they comfort me.

[5] You prepare a table before me in the presence of my enemies. You anoint my head with oil; my cup overflows.

[6] Surely your goodness and love will follow me all the days of my life, and I will dwell in the house of the Lord forever.

"The Lord is my shepherd"

Vacationing as a Sheep vs Vacation as a Shepherd

When I was growing up, traveling was simply a part of my life. My mom was a flight attendant, and because of that, we had the blessing of flying for free. Trips were constant throughout the years. Annual journeys to South Carolina to visit my father's side of the family, flights to Gary, Indiana, to see my mom's side, and plenty of other adventures sprinkled in-between. Most flights were within the United States, while some were international. But no matter where we went, my experience was the same, carefree.

As a kid, I didn't carry the weight of organizing for the trip or managing the logistics throughout. My role was simple: pack a bag, get on the plane, and enjoy the ride. I didn't think about where we would stay, how we would get from the airport to our destination, or what we would eat once we arrived. Those details were irrelevant to me. My childhood travel experiences were pure enjoyment from start to finish.

That changed with my first international trip as an adult. This was no ordinary trip; it was my honeymoon. My wife and I were heading to Jamaica, and for the first time, I wasn't just a passenger along for the ride. That trip placed me in the driver seat of our journey. The contrast from "along for the ride" to trip architect hit me immediately. Before we even left, there was so much to do: book the flights, reserve the hotel, figure out transportation, secure parking at the airport. I was responsible for making sure we had all the proper documents, passports, IDs, and reservation confirmations. I became painfully aware that one forgotten detail could unravel everything. If we miss a flight, lose a passport, or show up at the wrong terminal, the trip that launched our lifelong journey together could crumble.

Even after landing in Jamaica, the weight of my responsibilities didn't stop. I had fresh eyes to the world of travel: Do we have all our bags? Where's the driver I booked? Is this person trustworthy? Is this van safe? At the resort I had to consider, where are we going to eat? Is this the room I booked? Where do we go if someone gets sick or injured? Do they even take our insurance out here? How am I going to navigate a foreign country where everything from the culture to the crowds of people are unfamiliar? I felt like I was constantly on alert, my senses dialed up to ten anytime I stepped outside our hotel room. I realized I wasn't just a husband on his honeymoon. I was a protector, a planner, and a provider. My focus couldn't solely be on just enjoying my honeymoon, I also had the weight of making sure my wife was safe, comfortable, and cared for at all times.

One moment in particular is etched into my memory. We decided to leave the resort for an excursion to a local market. Everyone from our resort was eager to experience the local culture. We all piled into the execution bus and on we went. The bus dropped us off in front of a maze of merchant tents, twenty or thirty deep. The tents were all packed tightly together, each vendor calling out to the new batch of patrons, all eager for us to buy something from their tent. The sun was blazing, the crowd was thick, and as we walked deeper into the maze of tents, the pressure mounted. Many hands tugged at us, voices rose around us, and I could see the uneasiness building on my wife's face. There was no quick exit, no visible path out the maze of tents. I began to also feel my tension rise knowing that she was uncomfortable, and in that moment, I knew I had to do something. I grabbed her hand, put my shoulder forward, and carefully but firmly guided us back through the horde of people, retracing our steps until we made it back onto the excursion bus. Relief washed over her face, and with it, I felt my body finally exhale.

For the duration of the trip, I was in a heightened state of awareness. I never stopped scanning our surroundings, never stopped checking in on her. I bore the burden of ensuring not only her safety but also her peace and enjoyment. It was the first time I truly understood what it meant to travel as more than a carefree passenger.

During that trip, my eyes were opened. I recognized the responsibilities of travel that my parents carried all those years while I simply enjoyed our family trips without a worry. They were the ones orchestrating the plans, watching for dangers, and creating a safe space for me and my brother to simply experience the joys of the adventures. My gratitude for them grew a thousand-fold from that experience.

As we read the words of David in Psalm 23, we are drawn to pay attention to how the Holy Spirit inspired David to illustrate the connection of a shepherd and his sheep, while at the same time describing the vast different of their lived experiences. This duality of perspective came real to me through my travel experiences. That trip was a small glimpse of what life with God looks like; I am a sheep, and He is my Shepherd. As a child, I traveled as a sheep, with my parents taking on the shepherd role. But on my honeymoon trip I transitioned from being a sheep to a shepherd. I became the one to provide protection, stability, and peace. This is a miniscule analogy to the Lord's role as the Shepherd of our lives. God is the shepherd, he assumes this role, watching over us, providing for us, and carrying the weight of our safety and peace, often in ways we don't even realize.

As a child, I traveled in security because someone else carried the responsibility for me, just a sheep along for the ride. On my honeymoon, I felt the shift of obligation and needed to embrace the role of shepherd. But in life, no matter how much we try to plan, protect, and prepare, there is only one true Shepherd who shoulders the load of responsibility, and He never rests in His duty. The one who never misses a detail, who never leaves us unguarded or alone. The Lord is my Shepherd.

"The Lord is My Shepherd"

So, who is the Lord, what is a shepherd, and why is he mine?

To fully grasp this section of "The Lord is my Shepherd" in Psalm 23:1, there are three elements we must understand. *Who is the Lord? What is a shepherd? Why is He mine?* Let's examine each element and see how other scripture in the bible help us answer these questions.

Who is the Lord?

The Lord is... God -
Psalm 100:3 3 Know that the Lord is God. It is he who made us, and we are his; we are his people, the sheep of his pasture.

- From this verse, we see that the Lord and God are the same being. In the Hebrew language "Lord" is pronounced Yahweh or Jehovah. The "Lord" is the name that God discloses of himself in Exodus 3:14. The word "Lord" means "I Am Who I Am... I Am has sent me to you." In other words, "I Am" is the eternal supreme God. The name "Lord" is indeed God himself.

The Lord is... the good shepherd –
John 10:11-18 [11] I am the good shepherd. The good shepherd lays down his life for the sheep. [12] The hired hand is not the shepherd and does not own the sheep. So when he sees the wolf coming, he abandons the sheep and runs away. Then the wolf attacks the flock and scatters it. [13] The man runs away because he is a hired hand and cares nothing for the sheep. [14] "I am the good shepherd; I know my sheep and my sheep know me, [15] just as the Father knows me and I know the Father, and I lay down my life for the sheep. [16] I have other sheep that are not of this sheep pen. I must bring them also. They too will listen to my voice, and there shall be one flock and one shepherd. [17] The reason my Father loves me is that I lay down my life, only to take it up again. [18] No one takes it from me, but I lay it down of my own accord. I have authority to lay it down and authority to take it up again. This command I received from my Father."

- These are the actual words of Jesus, painting an intimate picture of who the Lord is. Jesus does this by describing the Lord through the metaphor of a shepherd, telling us; who the Lord is, what He does, His divine identity and character, and his relationship with humanity. These verses speak of his love for us, his sacrificial nature, sovereign power, and the unity between the Lord (Father) and Jesus. These verses centralize the core of the Gospel, which is God's love is sacrificial. "The Good shepherd lays down his life for the sheep." Unlike the hired hands who run when danger is present, The Good Shepherd Jesus faces the danger for His sheep. Our sin, death, and judgment, Jesus faces all for the sake of saving us, His people, His sheep. A mutual and intimate relationship between the shepherd and His sheep is stressed throughout these verses. It points us to the personal and relational closeness He desires to have with us. It also affirms the love and unity between Jesus and the Father, and God's plan for the redemption of His people.

The Lord is... the creator of all things -
Colossians 1:15-17 15 The Son is the image of the invisible God, the firstborn over all creation.16 For in him all things were created: things in heaven and on earth, visible and invisible, whether thrones or powers or rulers or authorities; all things have been created through him and for him. 17 He is before all things, and in him all things hold together.

- These verses communicate a profound and exalting description of who Jesus is as the Son in the Holy Trinity of God. These verses detail Jesus' preeminence to all things and His divine status. "In Him all things were created."

The Lord is... God the Father, God the Son, God the Holy Spirit: The Holy Trinity of God

* God the Father: The Author and originator of all
* God the Son: Our Savior, God incarnate
* God the Holy Spirit: The Helper

While the word "Trinity" does not appear in the Holy Bible manuscripts or the numerous translated versions. This truth is clearly and consistently taught throughout the holy scriptures. Very early and often in the Bible, it is clearly stated that there is only one God. "I am the Lord, and there is no other, apart from me there is no God" (Isaiah 45:5). We also see throughout the New Testament stories about the three distinct persons of God The Father (1 Corinthians 8:6), God the Son (John 1:1), and the God the Holy Spirit (2 Corinthians 3:17). It is God, himself, who discloses the mystery of himself in the Holy Trinity. He is the only God in three persons, who is co-equal, co-eternal, and co-existent in essence, in nature, in character, and in one perfect being. Jesus declares "I and the Father are one" (John 10:30). Jesus also proclaims, "I have much more to say to you... But when he, the Spirit of truth comes he will guide you into all truth (John 16:12). God the Father, God the Son, and God the Holy Spirit. An incomprehensible concept that can never be fully understood by humans, yet God gives us a glimpse of himself, a mystery of God, One in three, a Trinity in unity.

What is a shepherd?

The author of this Psalm was David. During this time, David was the King of Israel. Prior to his time as king, he was an actual shepherd. He was also the son of a shepherd. Therefore, David had first-hand knowledge of what it took to tend sheep. He knew what kept them healthy, what made them feel safe and at peace. He understood how to connect and speak to them so they would follow his command. His analogy in Psalm 23 of our relationship to God mirroring that of a shepherd to his sheep was a direct, intimate, lived experience of a shepherd. Yet, in this Psalm, David assumes the role of the sheep, placing the Lord in the role of the Shepherd. He speaks with a great sense of pride and adoration for his Shepherd. Clearly drawing this from his personal knowledge as a shepherd. David explains that the wellbeing of a sheep's life is solely dependent on its shepherd. With a good shepherd, a sheep can thrive and flourish in peace and harmony. In the care of a bad shepherd, a sheep will be on the verge of starvation, riddled with sickness and disease, relentlessly afraid, and in constant danger from predators ready to devour it as prey. Without debate our Lord as a Shepherd is the former.

Why is he mine?

David intentionally starts Psalm 23 by claiming the Lord as his shepherd. Fully understanding the obligations and duty of a shepherd to its flock. David takes claim to the Lord, confessing all that the Lord is doing in his life. The Shepherd is the defender and protector, leader and guide, supplier and provider, nurturer and comforter, steward and trustee, intercessor and martyr.

Isaiah 53:5 5But he was pierced for our transgressions, he was crushed for our iniquities; the punishment that brought us peace was on him, and by his wounds we are healed.

John 3:16 16 For God so loved the world that he gave his one and only Son, that whoever believes in him shall not perish but have eternal life."

It is God who desires and initiates a personal and intimate relationship with us. Fully demonstrated through the ultimate sacrifice of His only son to die for our sins and the sins of all the world. Jesus came to earth, lived a sinless life; he was tortured, and killed for our sins and transgressions. That act of selfless love, removed the barrier and permitted us to be reconciled to God, redeemed back to Him. "He is mine" because through the ultimate act of love He demonstrated that

I am His. Yet, the reality is, even greater than getting to say He is mine, is I get to say I AM HIS.

Summary

David's declaration in Psalm 23 "The Lord is my shepherd" is more than poetic imagery or a convenient analogy from his past career experience; it is a personal testimony of trust, belonging, and divine relationship. To proclaim the Lord as our Shepherd is to identify Him as our protector in danger, provider in lack, guide in confusion, and comforter in sorrow. A shepherd does not simply a watchman over their flock from a distance; they live among their sheep, leading them with care, and laying down their own life for the safety of their flock. That's exactly what the Lord has done.

Through the lens of Scripture, we understand the depth of this relationship. Isaiah 53:5 reveals that the punishment we deserved was placed on Christ, the Good Shepherd, who was pierced and crushed so we could walk in healing and peace. John 3:16 affirms the magnitude of God's love, sending His only Son so we might be saved and reconciled back into communion with Him. And Romans 5:8 reminds us that even in our sin, God loved us enough to pay the ultimate price.

So why is the Lord my shepherd? Because He chose me, saved me, and lives with me. He is not distant or indifferent. He is mine because through sacrifice, He made Himself mine. Even greater still: He is mine because, before I could ever say "He is mine," He looked at me, flawed and broken, and said, "You are mine."

PART II
Psalm 23

[1] The Lord is my shepherd, **I lack nothing.**

[2] He makes me lie down in green pastures, he leads me beside quiet waters,

[3] he refreshes my soul. He guides me along the right paths for his name's sake.

[4] Even though I walk through the darkest valley, I will fear no evil, for you are with me; your rod and your staff, they comfort me.

[5] You prepare a table before me in the presence of my enemies. You anoint my head with oil; my cup overflows.

[6] Surely your goodness and love will follow me all the days of my life, and I will dwell in the house of the Lord forever.

"I lack nothing"

Between the Gates and the Bus Stop

I grew up in Colorado, one of the top 5 economically diverse states in the country. My high school felt like a living snapshot of those statistics. Within a couple of miles in any direction, you could see two entirely different worlds. Walk a mile west of campus and you'd find yourself in a gated community lined with million-dollar homes, manicured lawns, backyard pools, and a clubhouse with gleaming tennis courts and polished hardwood basketball courts. Then, if you walked just two miles north, the scenery shifted. There, apartment complexes stood shoulder-to-shoulder, some subsidized, others bare-bones affordable housing. Families lived with less space and fewer resources, yet you could feel a different kind of energy pulsing through those streets.

The friends I made reflected that same spectrum. Take Jason, for example. He lived in that gated community. His family's house had six bedrooms, a three-car garages, a basement theater, a half-court basketball setup in the backyard, and a game room stocked like an arcade. When he drove to school in his new Jeep Grand Cherokee, it was hard not to think, *he lacked nothing*".

Then there was David. He lived in the other direction of the school than Jason and about 3 miles further away. His family lived in a two-bedroom apartment, his mom, three siblings, and him. You probably could have fit his whole place inside Jason's living room. Space was tight, and David was the oldest of his siblings, so most nights he would let his younger brothers sleep in in the bunkbeds that they had in their second bedroom, and his younger sister sleep on the pull-out couch. He would find a spot to blow up their air mattress and sleep in the living room. His mornings started with walking his siblings to their school, then catching a bus that dropped him a half mile from our school. From there, he hoofed it the rest of the way. From my young and naïve perspective, it seemed like a tough hand for a teenager to be dealt. But as I spent time with both Jason and David, my idea of "having it all" began to shift. The concept of lack or want evolved beyond just the material surface.

At Jason's house, everything you could imagine was within reach. He had a credit card from his parents and could order his way into whatever new gadget or gear caught his eye. After school we would often venture over to his house and his pantry looked like the shelves of a convenience store, chips, sodas, every kind of snack you could imagine. If I hung around long enough for dinner, we ordered takeout or delivery, no questions asked. At first, I thought it was the dream. The life every teen only dreamed about. Then, one afternoon, something struck me. After weeks of hanging out at Jason's, I realized I had never once seen his parents. Not even in passing on the way to the game room or when a delivery driver dropped off food. Finally, I asked.

"Yo, Jason, where are your parents at bro?"

Jason replied, *"Man, I don't know, somewhere out of town."*

"What!?! You and Sam (Jason's older brother) *are just here by yourselves?"* I asked with sheer disbelief.

"Yeah, man. They're always traveling for work." Jason stated as he carried on as if unbothered.

That answer stopped me cold. In my house, my parents barely let me and my older brother stay home alone when they went out for a dinner date, let alone for entire business trip out of the state. After that, I started noticing their absence everywhere: no one cheering him on at basketball games, no one at back-to-school night, no one at fundraisers. From the outside, Jason had every material thing a young adult could ask for. But did he really "lack nothing"?

David's home told a different story. His family ate breakfast and dinner together at the same table every morning and night. They prayed before bed together every night. David's mom and siblings filled the stands at every game, every concert, every activity. In that tiny apartment, you'd expect them to crave space from each other, but instead, their closeness seemed to be the glue holding them strong. David didn't have the latest sneakers or designer clothes. Sometimes he asked his mom for those things, but I never once heard him complain when the answer was no. He seemed settled and content with what he had.

From an external perspective, comparing Jason's and David's upbringings, one could easily conclude that Jason had it all. That he lacked for nothing. If we consider only the physical and material needs of this world, I would agree. But what about the non-physical? What about the intangible needs and desires that we crave? Desires like love, support, security, encouragement, peace of mind. The things that you cannot put a price tag on and receive with 1-day shipping from Amazon or DoorDash.

"I Lack Nothing"

Nothing? Really, nothing? In the King James version of the bible, this phrase is stated as "I shall not want". So, you are telling me that there are people who really want for nothing. To me, the word "want" goes beyond the notion of providing our most basic and fundamental needs of food, clothing, shelter, and safety. Those are needs not wants. Without food and water or safety, I can't even survive a night, but the new pair of Jordans, that nice North Face jacket online, a bigger house, or car, really anything that is not a need for survival would fall into the want category. It is easy to buy into the idea that God would provide the "needs" to His people. But the assertion 'I lack nothing' or "I shall not want" goes above and beyond basic needs, to wants, desires and dreams. It is a shepherd's duty to provide both the needs and wants for their sheep. Once again, In Psalm 23, David is speaking from the perspective of a sheep and this phrase, "I lack nothing or I shall not want," is the declaration of a sheep that is utterly and undoubtedly satisfied with the life that their owner has created for them. A sheep, David, perfectly content with its lot in life, that the Lord, the Good Shepherd, has provided. So, what truly is all encompassed in this lack/want for nothing?

What will you not lack?

The sentiment of lacking nothing goes far deeper than material provision. While physical needs like food, water, shelter, and clothing are included, this verse ultimately speaks to something beyond our carnal needs. This verse points to a life of spiritual sufficiency, relational security, and inner contentment found only in God's presence and care. A sheep is only at full contentment in the presence of the shepherd, and that peace and trust is created by the care the shepherd has provided. That contentment is mirrored on our relationship with the Lord our Good Shepherd. Throughout scripture two type of lack are addressed, physical & material lack, and spiritual lack. Let's take a look at how the Lord address these concepts.

Physical & material lack
Matthew 6:31-33 31 So do not worry, saying, 'What shall we eat?' or 'What shall we drink?' or 'What shall we wear?' 32 For the pagans run after all these things, and your heavenly Father knows that you need them. 33 But seek first his kingdom and his righteousness, and all these things will be given to you as well.

In Matthew, Jesus directly speaks about peoples' wants and desires for material things. He is communicating to his disciples about the worry and anxiety tied to the longing for material wants and the unfulfillment of life that comes from desiring after this world. Jesus then redirects their focus from the physical objects of desire to the spiritual provisions of life. Jesus proclaims that you need not to worry about anything, you will not lack these things, if you only turn your focus to the spiritual matters and "seek first his kingdom and righteousness".

From the very beginning, and throughout history, we hear stories and see evidence is presented about the God who provides for the needs for his people.

Genesis 22:14 14 So Abraham called that place, "Jehovah Jirah," which means "The Lord Will Provide." And to this day it is said, "On the mountain of the Lord it will be provided."

Exodus 16:4 4 Then the Lord said to Moses, "I will rain down bread from heaven for you. The people are to go out each day and gather enough for that day. In this way I will test them and see whether they will follow my instructions.

Deuteronomy 2:7 7 The Lord your God has blessed you in all the work of your hands. He has watched over your journey through this vast wilderness. These forty years the Lord your God has been with you, and you have not lacked anything.

Psalm 34:10 10 The lions may grow weak and hungry, but those who seek the Lord lack no good thing.

Matthew 7:9-11 9 "Which of you, if your son asks for bread, will give him a stone? 10 Or if he asks for a fish, will give him a snake? 11 If you, then, though you are evil, know how to give good gifts to your children, how much more will your Father in heaven give good gifts to those who ask him!

Spiritual lack

In Psalm 23, David speaks to what is beyond the physical and material needs of our every day lives. In the same way a good shepherd will provide everything its sheep need to live a prosperous life. The Lord our Shepherd, will provide our physical needs and more importantly the spiritual needs for His flock to prosper and thrive. These spiritual provisions of need include, Love, Peace, Joy, Guidance, Direction, and Protection.

Love: Belonging/Fellowship/Family
John 1:12 2Yet to all who did receive him, to those who believed in his name, he gave the right to become children of God

Galatians 3:26-27 [26]So in Christ Jesus you are all children of God through faith, [27]for all of you who were baptized into Christ have clothed yourselves with Christ.

1 John, 3:1 [1]See what great love the Father has lavished on us, that we should be called children of God! And that is what we are! The reason the world does not know us is that it did not know him.

Romans 8:14-17 [14] For those who are led by the Spirit of God are the children of God. [15] The Spirit you received does not make you slaves, so that you live in fear again; rather, the Spirit you received brought about your adoption to sonship. And by him we cry, "Abba, Father." [16] The Spirit himself testifies with our spirit that we are God's children. [17] Now if we are children, then we are heirs, heirs of God and co-heirs with Christ, if indeed we share in his sufferings in order that we may also share in his glory.

Peace

John 14:27 [27] Peace I leave with you; my peace I give you. I do not give to you as the world gives. Do not let your hearts be troubled and do not be afraid.

Philippians 4:7 [7] And the peace of God, which transcends all understanding, will guard your hearts and your minds in Christ Jesus.

Joy

Romans 15:13 [13] May the God of hope fill you with all joy and peace as you trust in him, so that you may overflow with hope by the power of the Holy Spirit.

John 15:11 [11] I have told you this so that my joy may be in you and that your joy may be complete.

Guidance and Direction
Proverbs 3:5-6 [5] Trust in the Lord with all your heart and lean not on your own understanding; [6] in all your ways submit to him, and he will make your paths straight.

Protection
Psalm 91:1-4 [1] Whoever dwells in the shelter of the Most High will rest in the shadow of the Almighty. [2] I will say of the Lord, "He is my refuge and my fortress, my God, in whom I trust." [3] Surely he will save you from the fowler's snare and from the deadly pestilence. [4] He will cover you with his feathers, and under his wings you will find refuge; his faithfulness will be your shield and rampart.

Proverbs 18:10 [10] The name of the Lord is a fortified tower; the righteous run to it and are safe.

Deuteronomy 31:6 [6] Be strong and courageous. Do not be afraid or terrified because of them, for the Lord your God goes with you; he will never leave you nor forsake you."

Summary

When David boldly affirms in Psalm 23, "I lack nothing" or "I shall not want", he is not speaking from a place of physical or material surplus or worldly wealth. He is speaking from the perspective of a sheep under the comprehensive and capable care of the Good Shepherd, God Himself. This is not a superficial claim, but a profound, abiding confidence that everything that is truly needed, physically, spiritually, emotionally, mentally, and relationally, is found in God and God alone.

David understood that lacking nothing meant more than having the tangible and physical needs, such as food, water, or shelter. He was making known the intangible provisions of walking in peace, knowing he was fully protected and cared for with great divine love by the Good Shepherd. He was making clear that because of his shepherd he received guidance when the path was unclear, joy in the midst of sorrow, and a secure identity as a beloved sheepy, or child of God. The Good Shepherd loves, leads, feeds, protects, stays with, and sacrifices for His flock. That is why David could say, without hesitation, "I lack nothing."

Ultimately, to lack nothing means to live in the steadfast truth that God is more than enough. When the Lord is your Shepherd, you are not left to fend for yourself. You are not abandoned to your own strength or understanding. You are fully seen, fully known, fully loved, and fully provided for. So, can you or I really lack nothing? The answer is a resounding YES, but only if and because we have Jesus, the Lord, our God, our Good Shepherd.

PART III
Psalm 23

1 The Lord is my shepherd, I lack nothing.

2 **He makes me lie down in green pastures**, he leads me beside quiet waters,

3 he refreshes my soul. He guides me along the right paths for his name's sake.

4 Even though I walk through the darkest valley, I will fear no evil, for you are with me; your rod and your staff, they comfort me.

5 You prepare a table before me in the presence of my enemies. You anoint my head with oil; my cup overflows.

6 Surely your goodness and love will follow me all the days of my life, and I will dwell in the house of the Lord forever.

"He makes me lie down in green pastures"

A few years back, I had the blessing to work as a coach at a Fellowship of Christian Athletes (FCA) sports camp. This was no small gathering. It brought together over 400 high school athletes and about 40 coaches from across Colorado for four days of competition, training, worship, and fellowship at the University of Northern Colorado.

Each sport had its specific group of athletes, and I was assigned to basketball. Our group was always one of the biggest groups, sometimes 70 to 90 players, with five or six coaches leading the charge. We practiced in the recreation center at the University, which held three full-size basketball courts under one roof. The moment 75+ athletes started dribbling at once, the place came alive with a deafening rhythm. Basketballs pounded the floor like a thunderstorm, sneakers squeaked, whistles blew, and voices shouted over all the noise. It was chaos, but a good kind of chaos, the kind that buzzes with energy and purpose.

One of the coaches on staff was a man we all called Coach Hawk. He had a three-year-old son who loved nothing more than to be in the gym with his dad. Wherever Coach Hawk went, his son followed, clutching his own mini basketball and mimicking every move like a tiny shadow. One afternoon, while Coach Hawk was in the middle of demonstrating a drill to the whole group, his wife walked into the gym carrying their son. His son's face was covered with streaks of tears. Coach Hawk glanced over and immediately took a quick pause. He proceeded to walk over to his wife. She handed their son over to Coach and said, "He just wants his daddy." Without hesitation, Coach Hawk took his son's small hand and led him back to the front of the group. Standing in front of nearly 80 teenagers, with every eye fixed on him, his son clung tightly to the back of his father's leg. He was clearly overwhelmed by the crowd, his little body pressed so firmly against his dad that Coach Hawk could hardly take a step.

Coach Hawk tried distracting him with a snack, and for a moment it worked, but that moment past and his son was back, clinging even harder, tears pooling in his eyes again. Crying once again, his son reached up with both hands gesturing for his father to pick him up. And so, right there in the middle of his demonstration, Coach Hawk scooped him up and continued coaching. His son tucked his little head tight against his dad's shoulder. The scene was out of a movie, a coach projecting his voice across a loud echoing gym, single arm raised to demonstrate drills, while at the same time carrying his little boy. As the session went on and the players broke into smaller groups to practice, the noise level rose even higher, balls were bouncing, shoes were squeaking, players laughter bouncing off the walls, other coaches' voices were shouting instructions, and in the middle of it all, I noticed something remarkable, Coach Hawk's son was nuzzled tightly against his father's shoulders had fallen fast asleep.

A young tiny child, sound asleep in his father's arms despite the chaos swirling around him. While the gym pulsed with noise and activity, he rested in complete peace. No fear, no worry, just the quiet trust that as long as he was in his father's arms, he was safe, secure, and at peace. Even in the midst of mayhem, solace and comfort was found in the loving embrace of father.

<h2 style="text-align:center">"He makes me lie down in green pastures"</h2>

Because sheep possess little to no means of self-defense, it is rare for them to lie down. Their only true defense mechanism of self-preservation is to flee. That being the case, it is uncommon for a sheep to lie down unless the external and internal conditions are precisely right. There are four conditions that must be met in order for sheep to lie down

1. They feel fully free of all fear
2. They are free from friction with the other sheep in the flock
3. They are free from the torment of parasites and flies
4. They are free from a sense of hunger or a desire to find food.

To lie down and rest, a sheep must be Free of FEAR, TENSION, AGGRAVATIONS, and HUNGER. The individual sheep is the only one that can determine if these criteria are met, and they are able to rest. But it is up to the Shepherd to provide the environment to enable this rest to occur. The shepherd and their diligent oversight of their sheep allows a sheep to feel a sense of peace and, in turn, lie down for rest. Let's take a deeper look at each of the 4 conditions for a sheep to lie down and assess how our Good Shepherd, the Lord, creates this environment for us to find peace and rest.

#1. Fully free of all fear

Fear often stems from things beyond our control. Worries and anxieties of what could be and what might happen can lead to fear. This fear can paralyze us from action and prevent us from stepping into what God has for our lives. The Bible frequently calls us to "not be afraid," or to be free of fear. This is not a baseless request for us to deny the true realities of this world and the presence of an enemy who desires to do nothing more than kill, steal, and destroy the children of God (John 10:10). But a calling to see beyond our daily realities, passed our worldly experiences and situations, and to look to the spiritual grounding in God's presence, promises, power, and His love. For a sheep, there is nothing greater than the presence of the shepherd in the pasture to remove fear and worry and create a sense of safety. The physical presence of the master/owner/protector can put a sheep at ease like nothing else can. The same presence of the Good Shepherd in our lives is how fear can be removed and we can experience peace.

Isaiah 41: 10 [10] So do not fear, for I am with you; do not be dismayed, for I am your God. I will strengthen you and help you; I will uphold you with my righteous right hand.

John 14: 16-17 [16] And I will ask the Father, and he will give you another advocate to help you and be with you forever [17] the Spirit of truth. The world cannot accept him, because it neither sees him nor knows him. But you know him, for he lives with you and will be in you.

Now, God does not promise us a life without danger or troubles, but he has promised us that we will never be alone. Thus, we do not need to fear during troubled and uncertain times, because His constant presence is our antidote to disarm our fear. Why is his presence the antidote? Because his presence comes with His power and His love. God is omnipresent (being present everywhere at the same time), omnipotent (having unlimited power; able to do anything), and all loving.

Isaiah 41:10 [10] So do not fear, for I am with you; do not be dismayed, for I am your God. I will strengthen you and help you; I will uphold you with my righteous right hand.

Jeremiah 32:17 [17] Ah, Sovereign Lord, you have made the heavens and the earth by your great power and outstretched arm. Nothing is too hard for you.

John 3:16 [16] For God so loved the world that he gave his one and only Son, that whoever believes in him shall not perish but have eternal life.

It seems like simple math to me: 1 + 1 + 1 will always equal 3. And...
God's Presence + God's Power + God's love = **Fully free of all fear**.

#2. Free from friction with others in their flock

Among all animal groupings, including humans, there is a natural order of control or status established. This is where we get the phrase "pecking order" referring to the positional rank amongst groups of chickens. Sheep display this same hierarchical behavior. They assert their dominance by butting and pushing other sheep away from the best grazing areas and places to rest or sleep. Each sheep unveils their dominance over the next, establishing the ranking order of dominance within the group. This constant battle for superiority amongst the flock causes tension and friction between the sheep. The entire herd becomes uneasy and cannot rest when a single sheep is jockeying for position; it creates a chain reaction of envy and competition for rank. This dynamic is no different in human beings. In any business, organization, sports team, friendship, or family, lies a battle for status. People constantly strive for approval and praise. They battle for a promotion, to be team captain, for awards of recognition, and for the attention of those who have positioned themselves at the top. This internal ambition turns into an external battle among each other, pursuing the top position or rank. In humans, this constant jockeying does not often manifest itself in butting and pushing like sheep, but in jealousy, backstabbing, discontentment, and even hatred towards one another. There is a constant friction created amongst ourselves because of our selfish self-ambitions to be at the "top-dog". This is not how God intended us to live our lives.

1 Timothy 6:6-8 6 But godliness with contentment is great gain. 7 For we brought nothing into the world, and we can take nothing out of it. 8 But if we have food and clothing, we will be content with that. 9 Those who want to get rich fall into temptation and a trap and into many foolish and harmful desires that plunge people into ruin and destruction.

So, the question becomes, how can we find contentment and peace with our lives and eliminate the friction and tension we create with others because of our ambitions to be on top? Within sheep, the primary factor that settles the flock and draws their attention away from their quarrels is the presence of the shepherd in the pasture. The shepherd's presence draws the attention of the sheep away from the self-assertions and establishes an environment of peace and satisfaction. Just like in the pasture, when our Good Shepherd is present in our lives, we can also find this contentment. The Bible shows us that true peace is only found in the presence of the Lord. His presence allows us to find contentment in our current circumstances, whatever that may be. His presence brings us security, calmness, and wholeness. For sheep to be "Free from friction with other sheep" the presence of the shepherd is necessary. For us to be free from tension with one another in our lives, we need the presence of the Good Shepherd.

Philippians 4:4-7 4Rejoice in the Lord always. I will say it again: Rejoice! 5 Let your gentleness be evident to all. The Lord is near. 6 Do not be anxious about anything, but in every situation, by prayer and petition, with thanksgiving, present your requests to God. 7 And the peace of God, which transcends all understanding, will guard your hearts and your minds in Christ Jesus.

#3. Free from torment of parasites and flies
One thing that a shepherd must be keenly aware of is the common behaviors of their sheep. These typical and common behaviors can be extremely altered by the presence of flies, tics, and other parasites. These irritants will eliminate any sense of calm or peace, making the sheep restless and reckless seeking relief. Sheep can be driven mad by these tormentors, making it impossible for them to find any sense of relief. They can be found stomping around the pasture, constantly shaking their heads, and rubbing their faces into the ground or bushes to find any relief available. Real relief from these nuisances can only be found from the shepherd's care. A good shepherd invests their time, money, and resources to mitigate these threats to their flock's peace. Various oils and ointments must be purchased and applied to each sheep's head, eyes, and ears. Equipment must be acquired and used to dip the sheep into insect repellent to cover and saturate their entire coat. Also, the shepherd must be attentive to their flock to notice when these tormentors are present, because they are not always visible to the human eye. A shepherd's keen senses and awareness of each sheep's behavior is essential in order to

provide prompt tactics for proactive protection or instance relief.

All people at times also experience annoyances and irritants from the world around us. Distractions pull our focus away from the peace and rest that our Good Shepherd provides. In John 17:27 Jesus said, 27 Peace I leave with you; my peace I give you. I do not give to you as the world gives. Do not let your hearts be troubled and do not be afraid.

We often allow external circumstances and worldly values to distract us from the peace and rest God has ordained for our lives. In today's world, technology, consumerism, and busyness are only some distractions that can rob us of this peace and rest.

Technology consumes many of our waking moments:
- Smartphones - Provide access for constant connectivity. We check emails, text messages, DMs, and any and all notifications. A full-fledged computer at our fingertips
- Social media sites – The breeding ground for comparison culture, fostering insecurity, envy, self-doubt, and shame. Even when things are going great, it seems to be never enough.
- On-demand television provides access to whatever a person might want to watch, whenever they want it. Access to an endless number of shows, movies, and games to keep us distracted and occupied around the clock.
- Video games - glamourize some of the world's most disturbing realities and numb us to real-world atrocities that can desensitize us to violence and pain.

Consumerism & Materialism, shifts our focus from inner fulfillment with the Lord to convincing ourselves we need more to be happy and satisfied

- More money, more possessions, more success - A cycle of chronic dissatisfaction and a sense to "keep up with the Jones'"
- Our identity becomes associated with our "things", and when we get caught up in finding our value in the things that we have, we lose the identity that we have in Christ. We can go from being children of God who are reborn by faith in Jesus, chosen, forgiven, and reconciled to have peace with God, to feeling that we are not enough, insufficient, insecure, and unworthy.

Busyness keeps our minds and bodies in a constant state of activity, leaving little to no time and space for reflection, stillness, and connection with our Lord

- In many cultures, especially American culture, busyness and work are equated to success. People wear busyness as a badge of honor. Coming in early and staying late are equated to commitment and determination. Even more alarming, a recent study showed that the majority of workers in the US and Canada perform work tasks while on vacation. Because of this busyness culture mindset, we begin to believe that we are only valuable when we are doing something, instead of finding our identity and value in who we are in Christ.

Just as a good shepherd must diligently care for his sheep to protect them from parasites and other insect irritants, our Good Shepherd, offers us protection and peace from the irritants and tormentors in our world today. The human "parasites" of need for constant digital connectivity, social media comparison, consumerism, and a culture of busyness, all distract our focus from the lasting peace found in Christ alone, and rob us of our peace, while stirring anxiety, and ill health. True rest and peace are only possible when we remain under the attentive care of our Good Shepherd, who invites us to step away from worldly chaos and abide in His stillness, presence, and love. This is achieved through intentional action of connection. The Lord is always ready and willing to connect. Simple acts like, reading and studying God's word daily, finding regular time for prayer and meditation with the Lord, giving His thanks or praise throughout your day, or finding a community of believes to live out your life with are all small ways to live in his presence daily.

#4. Free from a sense of hunger

"Green pastures" are the key to sheep's dietary satisfaction. The previous three conditions required for a sheep to find the peace and rest to lie down are internal to the sheep. "Green pastures" are about the external environment of the sheep. The agricultural surroundings of the sheep govern its ability to feed and rest. A lush green pasture allows for quick eating and fulfillment, but a dry pasture requires constant searching for food and the nutrients needed. A shepherd not only has to be entuned and attentive to the behaviors of its sheep but also well versed in the environment that is necessary for flourishing. Tremendous time, labor, and agricultural knowledge and skill are needed to produce green pastures. Clearing of rough & rocky land, deep plowing, soil preparation, seeding, planting, proper irrigating and watering, are all vital components to a lush, well-maintained pasture.

We as humas have multiple environments that our Good Shepherd is keenly attentive to. We have a physical environment, an internal environment, and a spiritual environment. He diligently works to keep each environment green and plush enabling our ability to live and thrive. He is constantly clearing the rocks of doubt and unbelief from our thoughts and circumstances. He is plowing deeply into the fields of our spirits in order to uproot our sin and preparing our soil for His Holy Spirit. He is sowing the seeds of grace and His Word in our hearts and planting it into our minds to take root and to grow throughout all aspects of our lives. He is constantly watering us with the presence of His Holy Spirit in order to produce the optimal environment for our peace and rest.

Summary

"He makes me lie down in green pastures..." This simple phrase paints a picture of serenity, but behind the stillness is the diligent and intentional work of a loving Shepherd. This image of a sheep lying down in green pastures is not one of passivity or indifference, it is a profound declaration of trust, security, and contentment. For a sheep to lie down, all sources of tension, fear, irritation, and hunger must be removed. The only one who can create that environment is the shepherd. In the same way, we as God's children only obtain true rest under the attentive, loving, and powerful care of our Good Shepherd, the Lord. The Lord does not just suggest we rest; He and He alone make it possible.

In our chaotic and demanding world, fear threatens our peace, conflict steals our joy, daily frustrations torment our minds, and constant striving leaves our souls malnourished. In a world that constantly drives us to do more, achieve more, and carry more, the Lord offers something radically different in green plush pastures. Just as a faithful shepherd removes every barrier to rest for his flock, so our Savior steps into our lives, not just to manage our problems, but to transform the very atmosphere of our existence. He doesn't offer shallow solutions or quick fixes. He offers Himself.

- **He removes fear** through His presence, power, and perfect love.
- **He settles our internal battles** and external tensions with His peace that surpasses understanding.
- **He soothes our irritations** by applying the oil of His Spirit to our minds and hearts.
- **He nourishes our souls** by planting and growing the truth of His Word in us.

The green pastures of Psalm 23 are not just about abundance; they are about divine preparation. A place carefully cultivated by the Good Shepherd where His sheep can truly rest, flourish, and dwell in peace. And so, we are reminded that in times of need rest and comfort, we don't have to make ourselves lie down. He provides the tranquil environment so we can peacefully lie down. He takes the lead. He does the work. Our role is simply to trust, to stay close, and to allow ourselves to rest under His divine eternal care.

PART IV
Psalm 23

¹ The Lord is my shepherd, I lack nothing.

² He makes me lie down in green pastures, **he leads me beside quiet waters,**

³ he refreshes my soul. He guides me along the right paths for his name's sake.

⁴ Even though I walk through the darkest valley, I will fear no evil, for you are with me; your rod and your staff, they comfort me.

⁵ You prepare a table before me in the presence of my enemies. You anoint my head with oil; my cup overflows.

⁶ Surely your goodness and love will follow me all the days of my life, and I will dwell in the house of the Lord forever.

"he leads me beside quiet waters,"

From Printouts to Peace of Mind: The Third Wheel on Our Anniversary Trip

For my wife and I one-year anniversary, we decided to celebrate with a trip to Costa Rica. At the time, driving navigation looked very different. This was before GPS navigation came standard on every smartphone and in the dash of most vehicles. Sure, a few people had those clunky Garmin or TomTom units that you could plug into the cigarette lighter of your car, but most of us relied on MapQuest. You'd sit at the computer, type in your starting point and destination, and print off 15 total pages of the turn-by-turn directions (at least half of the pages were just random ads). These directions listed the street names to turn; the distances you would travel before that turn and the turning direction. All the information one needed to get from place to place. We used to carry those sheets of paper in our cars like they were gold. That was the plan I had in place.

Costa Rica has two main international airports: Juan Santamaria International in San José, and Daniel Oduber Quirós International in Liberia. Our hotel was in Liberia, but flights into San José were much cheaper, so I figured we'd save a little money by flying into San José and then making the four-and-a-half-hour drive across the country to our hotel. I thought it was a pretty solid plan, save some money and see more of Costa Rica's beautiful country by car.

When we landed in San José, we got our bags, went through customs, and headed to the rental car location. After filling out the paperwork, the agent asked if I wanted to add a GPS system to the rental.

"How much is it?" I asked

"$34 per day."

"Per day?!" I almost audible laughed when I heard his response.

The agent nodded matter-of-factly.

I shook my head. *"No, I'm good. Thank you though."*

The whole point of flying into San José was to save money, and I wasn't about to hand it right back just for directions. I had my trusty stack of MapQuest printouts, and with my wife riding shotgun as the navigator, I felt confident enough to take on the challenge.

We climbed into the car, adjusted our seats, and took a deep breath before pulling out of the lot. My wife read off the first street, then the next turn. Easy enough. But within minutes, we realized we had a major problem. Costa Rica didn't have any street sign showing the streets names. Not in the way we were used to back home. We drove past block after block, intersections with traffic lights, roundabouts with exits, but no street signs. Not one! The entire foundation of my carefully printed MapQuest directions crumbled within the first 2 minutes of our journey. How in the world were we supposed to drive 150 miles across a foreign country using directions based on street names, without any signs to indicate the streets?

It didn't take long for me to swallow my pride and turn the car around and head back to the rental agency. Back at the rental counter, I pulled my card, place in on the counter and said,

"We'll take the GPS." Suddenly, that $34-a-day price tag didn't seem so outrageous.

From that point forward, our trip transformed. The GPS became like the third member of our vacation. It calmly guided us with the quickest and easiest route to our destination. Verbal and visual step-by-step instructions, around traffic jams, detoured us through construction zones, and rerouted us when accidents blocked the street. We had a clear, confident voice leading us through the chaos.

One afternoon, we decided to explore a beach away from our hotel. I input the address, and the GPS cheerfully announced that we'd be there in 22 minutes. Perfect, I thought to myself. We followed its guidance until it led us off the paved road and straight toward what looked like a path into the rainforest. We were no longer on a road at all, more like a trail carved out by the native animal life. I hesitated, staring at the thick trees and the rocky ground ahead. "There's no way this is right," I said.

Not wanting to chance it, I asked the GPS for an alternative route. It recalculated and sent us back toward the highway. The new estimated trip duration was two hours and thirty minutes.

We sat there for a moment, weighing our options: two and a half hours on a paved but winding road, or 22 minutes through the unknown. My wife looked at me, and I could tell she was thinking the same thing I was. We had come all this way for an adventure, so why not?

We eased forward onto the path. The road was rough and narrow, weaving through dense green forest, over rocks, and up steep hills. At times, it felt like the car might tip if we were both to lean to the same side of the car. My hands gripped the wheel tighter with each bump, but then, after what felt like a wild ride through a movie scene, the trees opened up, and there it was, a stunning stretch of white sand beach, waves rolling in, and sunlight glinting off the water. Just like the GPS promised, we had arrived in 22 minutes.

From then on, I didn't question the little device. What started as an overpriced add-on became our lifeline, guiding us safely through an unfamiliar country. It turned what could have been a stressful, frustrating trip into an adventure we could actually enjoy. With the GPS, we weren't just surviving the trip, we were soaking in the beauty of Costa Rica, at peace, free to explore without fear.

That GPS wasn't just technology, for those four days, it was our comfort, our guide, and our quiet assurance that no matter where we ended up, even if in the middle of a rainforest path, we'd make it safely to our destination and in the shortest time possible.

"He leads me beside quiet waters"

Sheep can live in a variety of conditions, even in very dry and desolate climates, however, clean and plentiful water sources are essential for their survival. It is up to the shepherd to find and provide these necessary conditions for their flock. It is with much diligence and effort that the shepherd must lead their flock to the best watering sources if they want them to thrive and flourish. Without the shepherd, sheep will drink from any available pool of water regardless of if contaminated, or polluted. These unsanitary types of water sources can be filled with parasites, harmful bacteria, and toxins, which can lead to illness or death.

Coincidentally we find this same pattern in human behavior. If we are not properly led, we search for and consume any source to quench our thirst. We do have a physical thirst for water, but I am referring to our thirst for fulfillment. This thirst is a deep, intrinsic, and persistent longing to live a life of meaning and purpose. It reflects our internal drive to feel valued, connected, and content, not just in what we do but who we are. This thirst goes beyond mere basic survival needs such as food, water, and shelter, but a desire to know that our lives have meaning, and that we are seen, loved, and we are making a difference in the world around us. Men, women, and children alike, constantly strive for these fulfillments. This internal fulfillment is often manifested through the concepts of affirmation, gratification, acceptance, and belonging. These longings can either be filled in a positive way, through an intimate relationship with the Lord, our Good Shepherd, or they can be fulfilled by worldly means that only provide a temporary and false sense of fulfillment. Let's examine how our thirsts can be fulfilled, by the world or by the Good Shepherd.

Affirmation

Worldly fulfillment: Worldly affirmations are found through superficial means such as likes and followers on social media. Many find personal worth and validation in what they are able to show off to others, thinking others will value them by what they have. Possessions like luxury cars, designer clothes, or expensive gadgets can be seen as the epitome of success that leads others to admire or envy the owner. These false external validations begin to feel like personal affirmation. Worldly fulfillments for affirmation can also be falsely found in physical appearance. Individuals derive a sense of self-worth, confidence, or identity based on how they look and how they feel others respond to their appearance.

Fulfillment through the Good Shepherd: The Bible teaches us that true affirmation and identity can only come from God, our creator and redeemer. We need to look no further than Jesus to realize that we are loved; we are cared for; and we are enough because Jesus meets us just where we are.

Isaiah 43:1-7 [1]But now, this is what the Lord says he who created you, Jacob, he who formed you, Israel: "Do not fear, for I have redeemed you; I have summoned you by name; you are mine. [2] When you pass through the waters, I will be with you; and when you pass through the rivers, they will not sweep over you. When you walk through the fire, you will not be burned; the flames will not set you ablaze. [3] For I am the Lord your God, the Holy One of Israel, your Savior; I give Egypt for your ransom, Cush and Seba in your stead. [4] Since you are precious and honored in my sight, and because I love you, I will give people in exchange for you, nations in exchange for your life. [5] Do not be afraid, for I am with you; I will bring your children from the east and gather you from the west. [6] I will say to the north, 'Give them up!' and to the south, 'Do not hold them back.'
Bring my sons from afar and my daughters from the ends of the earth [7] everyone who is called by my name, whom I created for my glory, whom I formed and made."

Gratification

Worldly fulfillment: Gratification is defined as *pleasure, especially when gained from the satisfaction of a desire.* The desire for worldly pleasure can easily become misaligned with what truly matters. This misalignment turns the focus to self-gratification. We become self-centered, excessive, or disconnected from deeper purpose. Self-gratification ultimately leads to destructive actions for attainment. These worldly desires and pleasures are found in devastating vices like pornography, drugs and alcohol, and even overeating. Temporary fixes for unmet desires can lead to unfulfillment, depression, and even death.

Fulfillment through the Good Shepherd: The Bible teaches us that all our desires, wants, and needs can be met through Jesus Christ our Lord. True gratification, lasting joy and fulfillment, is found in God's presence and purpose for our lives.

Psalms 16:1-11 1 Keep me safe, my God, for in you I take refuge. 2 I say to the Lord, "You are my Lord; apart from you I have no good thing." 3 I say of the holy people who are in the land, "They are the noble ones in whom is all my delight." 4 Those who run after other gods will suffer more and more. I will not pour out libations of blood to such gods or take up their names on my lips. 5 Lord, you alone are my portion and my cup; you make my lot secure. 6 The boundary lines have fallen for me in pleasant places; surely, I have a delightful inheritance. 7 I will praise the Lord, who counsels me; even at night my heart instructs me. 8 I keep my eyes always on the Lord. With him at my right hand, I will not be shaken. 9 Therefore my heart is glad, and my tongue rejoices; my body also will rest secure, ¹⁰ because you will not abandon me to the realm of the dead, nor will you let your faithful one see decay. ¹¹ You make known to me the path of life; you will fill me with joy in your presence, with eternal pleasures at your right hand.

Acceptance & Belonging

While the world often offers a flickering, conditional sense of community, scripture suggests that our deepest ache for belonging is actually a "homesickness" for our creator. True acceptance isn't found in meeting earthly standards, but in the reality which states that God "predestined us for adoption" into His own family. This relationship with God shifts our identity from spiritual orphans to "children of God" (John 1:12), providing a security that doesn't fluctuate with our performance. When we anchor ourselves in the Heavenly Father, we find we are no longer searching for a place to fit in; rather, we are settling into our status as a "chosen people" (1 Peter 2:9), fully known and permanently loved.

Biblical Truths and Scriptural confirmation

God's acceptance comes from his grace, by faith, and not our performance

Ephesians 1:4-6 ⁴ For he chose us in him before the creation of the world to be holy and blameless in his sight. In love ⁵ he predestined us for adoption to sonship through Jesus Christ, in accordance with his pleasure and will, ⁶ to the praise of his glorious grace, which he has freely given us in the One he loves.

The world's acceptance is temporary and misleading

1 John 2:15-17 ¹⁵ Do not love the world or anything in the world. If anyone loves the world, love for the Father is not in them. ¹⁶ For everything in the world, the lust of the flesh, the lust of the eyes, and the pride of life, comes not from the Father but from the world. ¹⁷ The world and its desires pass away, but whoever does the will of God lives forever.

God's love provides everlasting acceptance
Romans 8:38-39 ³⁸ For I am convinced that neither death nor life, neither angels nor demons, neither the present nor the future, nor any powers, ³⁹ neither height nor depth, nor anything else in all creation, will be able to separate us from the love of God that is in Christ Jesus our Lord.

Summary

Just as sheep rely on the shepherd to guide them to clean, life-sustaining water, we too depend on our Good Shepherd, the Lord, to lead us to sources that truly satisfy the deep thirsts of our souls. Our intrinsic longing for affirmation, gratification, and acceptance mirrors the sheep's dependence. Without direction, we risk quenching our thirst from polluted, dangerous sources that offer only temporary relief, false perception, and excessive harm. But when we follow the voice of the Shepherd, He leads us to "quiet waters" places of peace, wholeness, and eternal truth.

In a world filled with counterfeit fulfillments, social validation, materialism, performance-based worth, and fleeting pleasures, God invites us to something far greater. He offers, internal fulfillment and affirmation through His Word, soul-deep satisfaction in His presence, and unconditional acceptance. A resounding truth that we belong to him and that he belongs to us by His grace through faith. As Psalm 23 assures us, we are not wandering alone. We are being led, patiently, lovingly, and purposefully to places where our souls can truly drink, rest, be restored, and flourish.

Let us not settle for the world's water. Although the worldly listen to the voices of today and are drawn to what may seem like gold. What sparkles for a while, will tarnish, rust and pass away with time. Instead, let us wait on the Lord, listen for the Good Shepherd's voice and follow Him faithfully to the still, clean, pure, quiet waters of His perfect provision.

John 4:13-14 13 Jesus answered, "Everyone who drinks this water will be thirsty again, 14 but whoever drinks the water I give them will never thirst. Indeed, the water I give them will become in them a spring of water welling up to eternal life."

PART V
Psalm 23

1 The Lord is my shepherd, I lack nothing.

2 He makes me lie down in green pastures, he leads me beside quiet waters,

3 **he refreshes my soul**. He guides me along the right paths for his name's sake.

4 Even though I walk through the darkest valley, I will fear no evil, for you are with me; your rod and your staff, they comfort me.

5 You prepare a table before me in the presence of my enemies. You anoint my head with oil; my cup overflows.

6 Surely your goodness and love will follow me all the days of my life, and I will dwell in the house of the Lord forever.

"he refreshes my soul."

The longest timeout

For as long as I can remember, sports have been a major part of my life. I joined my first team at five years old, running around on a pee-wee soccer field with shin guards too big for my legs and a jersey that practically hung to my knees. From there it was one season after another. I played tee-ball in the spring, basketball in the winter, coach pitch and baseball in the summer, a few years of football, track meets in between, and even karate lessons squeezed into the mix. Looking back, I can't recall a single stretch of time in my childhood when I wasn't a part of a sports team. Competing, learning, creating lifelong friendships and growing through sports.

But among all those activities, one rose above the rest, basketball. From the moment I first held a ball, I was hooked. It wasn't just a game; it became the rhythm of my days. I'd shoot baskets in the driveway before school and dribble my ball to the bus stop before throwing it in my backpack for the day. At lunch, you could find me on the blacktop, engaged in intense pickup games with my friends. After school, I was either at team practice or putting up shots until the sky turned dark. I can still hear my mom's voice, "T, come in for dinner". Basketball was more than my favorite sport; it was my anchor.

It became the place I turned to when life felt heavy. If I was frustrated or sad, I'd go dribble and shoot until the sound of the ball hitting the rim drowned out the noise in my head. If I was nervous about school or anxious about talking to a girl, the court was where my nerves settled down. Basketball was my peace, a refuge I could always count on.

That love for the game carried me all the way to college where I was blessed with the privilege of playing basketball at the University of Northern Colorado. But during the fall of my senior year, everything shifted in one ordinary moment.

We were in the middle of conditioning workouts, running sprint and agility drills. It was nothing new, just explosive starts, quick stops, pushing ourselves like we always did. On my third rep, I pushed off hard, sprinted a few strides, and then it happened, a sharp pop in the back of my leg stopped me cold. At first, I thought maybe it was just a cramp or a tweak, but when I slowed to a limp and sat down, the reality began to set in.

I hobbled over to our athletic trainer. He checked a few things and then looked at me with that serious expression athletes know all too well. "Well, T, it looks like you might have pulled your hamstring." My heart dropped. "So, what does that mean?" I asked, hoping it was not something serious. He said, "You're going to have to stay off that leg and the court. No basketball for at least three to four weeks. Then we'll reevaluate."

Three to four weeks might as well have been three to four years. At that point in my life, I hadn't gone more than a few days without basketball. I remembered once in high school, my family planned a three-day cruise. I told my mom I wouldn't go unless she let me bring my basketball. That was how deep the game ran in me, and now I was being told I couldn't play at all.

Those weeks were brutal. The physical pain was nothing compared to the emotional toll. I'd sit in the gym during practice, watching my teammates run drills and scrimmage, while I stayed stuck on the sideline with ice and heating packs.

I felt like I had lost a part of myself. My motivation to go to class faded. I didn't want to hang out with friends. I was withdrawn, restless, and empty. I was Popeye without his spinach, Thor without his hammer.

When the trainer finally cleared me to play basketball again, it was like a rebirth. The first time I stepped back onto the court for practice, ball in hand, it felt like taking a long drink of ice water after crossing a desert. Every dribble, every shot, every bead of sweat was a reminder that I was back where I belonged. The hunger returned. The fire came alive again.

That injury taught me something that I didn't fully grasp until then: just how much the game meant to me. Losing basketball, even for a short time, revealed its true value in my life, not just as a sport, but as a part of who I am. And when I got it back, it revitalized me. I was refreshed, mind, body, and soul.

"He Refreshes My Soul"

In Psalm 23, David moves from describing the green pastures and the physical rest the pasture provides, to a deep internal renewal, "He refreshes my soul." This refreshing goes far beyond the invigorating feeling of running through the sprinklers as a kid on a 100-degree day. This refresh is the complete restoration and rejuvenation of our innermost being. A revitalization when we are lost, worn down, or broken.

The Hebrew word for "refreshes" is "Shuv". Shuv is a verb, a word of action that carries the meaning of "to return, to bring back, to restore to the original state". Sheep, much like people, are prone to depletion. The journey of life is not always smooth and lush. We all experience seasons of strain and frustration that deplete our strength. We experience stretches of wandering that remove our joy, and times of failure and lack that make us question our faith. Try to picture a lost, confused, exhausted, or injured sheep. During these times, it is the shepherd that must persistently search, find, and rescue. It is on the shepherd, to bring the sheep back safely, nurse injuries, or provide nourishing water and restore peace. Our Father and Good Shepherd mirrors this heroism. When we feel the shame and guilt of our sin, heartbroken by the loss of a loved one, lost to addiction, or in fear because of the lack of worldly affirmation, our Good Shepherd does not merely patch us up to keep us moving. He draws us into His heavenly care and protection and restores us back to peace in His presence and love. In the care of the Good Shepherd, our souls are refreshed, and this is both a promise of God and a process alongside Him. We need our soul to be refreshed for a variety of reasons. We may all have different paths and journeys in life, but we all experience missteps and stumbles that knock us off our path. When we are off balance we need our Good Shepherd's refreshing.

He Brings Us Back When We Wander
It is very common for sheep to wander away from their flock. They are typically drawn away by distractions like patches of grass that appear greener from a distance, distant pools of water to drink, or shady areas for rest. During these times of wandering, they can easily become "cast down". Cast down is a term that describes when a sheep has fallen on its backs and cannot roll back over to their feet. When sheep become cast down, they cannot get up without assistance, which typically comes in the form of their shepherd. A cast sheep is vulnerable to predators, starvation, and death unless the shepherd returns it to its upright nature quickly.

As people, we too are inclined to wander. We are often distracted by the cares and pleasures of the world and in turn, we neglect God's Word. These distractions lead us to sin against God, and spiritually drift away, leaving us "cast down." In spite of our roaming ways, the Good Shepherd seeks out those who stray and draws them from helplessness. The Good Shepherd returns us upright, bringing us back into His tender care. It is important to note, bringing back is not done through punishment and shame, but through his grace, love and compassion, for us.

Isaiah 53:6 6 We all, like sheep, have gone astray, each of us has turned to our own way; and the Lord has laid on him the iniquity of us all.

Luke 15: 4-6 4 "Suppose one of you has a hundred sheep and loses one of them. Doesn't he leave the ninety-nine in the open country and go after the lost sheep until he finds it? 5 And when he finds it, he joyfully puts it on his shoulders 6 and goes home. Then he calls his friends and neighbors together and says, 'Rejoice with me; I have found my lost sheep.'"

We may find ourselves "cast down", lost, and wandering through life at times, but through the grace and strength of the Father, he diligently searches for us to restore and refresh our souls. Just as a shepherd rejoices over a recovered sheep, our Lord delights in restoring us to Himself. In His loving hands, every wandering soul finds its way back to safety, peace, and purpose.

He Heals What Is Broken

A shepherd's care for their sheep includes tending to injuries such as cuts from thorns, bruises from falls, infections, and broken bones. If left unattended, these injuries, big or small, can lead to infection and death. The shepherd must take the time to frequently inspect each sheep, clean wounds, apply oil or ointment, and bind or patch exposed wounds until they heal.

As humans, our souls can also bear wounds. Emotional scars, broken trusts, griefs from loss, and pains of regret. Some wounds are self-inflicted through internalized self-criticism, guilt, and regret from personal choices or unresolved shame. While other wounds come from external means, like acts of injustice, dehumanization, oppression, and the cruelty of other people. In either scenario, if these wounds are left untreated, they will harden our hearts to be bitter, in despair, hopeless, cynical, or depressed, causing unhealthy coping mechanisms, distorted beliefs, or poor decisions that we later regret. Still, our Good Shepherd is attentive and caring. He is aware of every pain and hurt. He is ready to apply the healing balm of His Spirit and His Word to all our scars and wounds. In His presence, no wound is too deep, and no hurt is too hidden. He to clean our wounds and restore us better than ever before. His healing work transforms our pain into testimonies of His grace. When we allow the Good Shepherd to tend to our brokenness, our soul is refreshed. This refreshment is not just about feeling better; it's about being our best, who God created us to be. Through His refresh, we are made whole in body, spirit and soul.

Matthew 11:28-29 [28] Come to me, all you who are weary and burdened, and I will give you rest. [29] Take my yoke upon you

and learn from me, for I am gentle and humble in heart, and
you will find rest for your souls.

He Restores Joy and Strength

Sheep that are hungry, thirsty, or malnourished cannot thrive.
A wise shepherd leads them to fresh water and lush grazing
land, not only to sustain them but to renew their vitality. In
the same way, our souls can become spiritually malnourished,
running on empty. When we feed on what the world offers as
sustenance and deprive ourselves of spiritual nutrients, that
come graciously from the Word of God we become
malnourished. The lack of spiritual sustenance is manifested
in many different areas of our lives. We begin to lose joy and
peace, and in turn we can feel anxiety, confusion, and
restlessness. We also become susceptible to temptation,
deception, and fall into sin. But just like a sheep, our Good
Shepherd is continually trying to bring us back, fully knowing
what harm can come from seeking nutrition outside of
Him. Our Good Shepherd is always ready to bring us back to
the living water of His presence and the nourishing truth of
His Word. We must simply be willing to surrender to His care.
When the Good Shepherd refreshes our souls, He replaces our
depletion with His strength, our despair with His joy, and our
weariness with His endurance.

Isaiah 40:31 [31]But those who hope in the LORD will renew
their strength. They will soar on wings like eagles; they will
run and not grow weary; they will walk and not be faint.

He Renews Our Purpose

Seasons of failure or fatigue can cause us to forget why we
were created and we abandon the assignments that God has
given us, our true purpose. In a similar fashion, a cast down or

wandering sheep does not benefit the shepherd or the flock. But a refreshed and restored sheep thrives again and is able to follow the shepherd and contribute to the well-being of all the sheep in the flock. In the same way, the Good Shepherd longs to refresh our souls and restore our sense of purpose. Through restoration, the Good Shepherd instills fresh purpose into us, reminding us that we are His workmanship, created in Christ Jesus to do good works, which God prepared in advance for us to do (Ephesians 2:10). The refreshment He provides is not just to comfort us but to re-commission us, His refreshing is our factory reset.

Ephesians 2:8-10 [8] For it is by grace you have been saved, through faith, and this is not from yourselves, it is the gift of God, [9] not by works, so that no one can boast. [10] For we are God's handiwork, created in Christ Jesus to do good works, which God prepared in advance for us to do.

Psalm 51:10-12 [10] Create in me a pure heart, O God, and renew a steadfast spirit within me. [11] Do not cast me from your presence or take your Holy Spirit from me. [12] Restore to me the joy of your salvation and grant me a willing spirit, to sustain me.

Summary

"He refreshes my soul" is the testimony of every sheep who has felt the hands of the Shepherd lift them from their weariness, cleanse their wounds, and set them back on the right path. It is not a momentary relief, but a deep, life-giving renewal that touches every part of who we are.

Our Good Shepherd refreshes us when we wander, heals us when we are broken, strengthens us when we are weak, and renews our sense of purpose. His refreshment is not earned, bought, deserved, or won, but freely given through God's grace.

The world may offer temporary distractions, quick fixes, and surface-level relief and refreshment, but only the Lord offers true restoration. When our souls are depleted, the answer is not to push harder or to try to fix ourselves; it is to simply surrender to the Father, and he will do the rest. He is both the source and the sustainer of our refreshment.

PART VI
Psalm 23 (NIV)

¹ The Lord is my shepherd, I lack nothing.

² He makes me lie down in green pastures, he leads me beside quiet waters,

³ he refreshes my soul. **He guides me along the right paths for his name's sake.**

⁴ Even though I walk through the darkest valley, I will fear no evil, for you are with me; your rod and your staff, they comfort me.

⁵ You prepare a table before me in the presence of my enemies. You anoint my head with oil; my cup overflows.

⁶ Surely your goodness and love will follow me all the days of my life, and I will dwell in the house of the Lord forever.

"He guides me along the right paths for his name's sake."

The Best Desert in History

I don't mean to brag, but without question, hesitation, beyond a shadow of a doubt, there is no contest, and any other competitive phrase you can think of, my Granny made the best dessert EVER in the history of the world. I'm pretty sure that's a historical fact, if I'm not mistaken. This incredibly delicious dessert was her vanilla pound cake. Even now, my mouth waters just thinking about it.

It wasn't just *a* cake. It was *the* cake. This pound cake was soft and dense, moist on the inside, and was covered with a perfectly textured golden-brown crust. It was sweet, but never too sweet, buttery in every bite, and topped with just the right amount of vanilla icing drizzle that was precisely cascaded gently down the sides. If you want to know what it tasted like, close your eyes and imagine your very first bite of dessert in heaven, that's about as close as words can describe.

Of course, Granny's pound cake wasn't something she whipped up every week. No, it was reserved for special occasions, birthdays, holidays, reunions, those moments where family gathered and memories were made. Her baking method was not something quick and simple, like the cakes you can make from a box. It was a full-fledged process, almost a ceremony of sorts. Every ingredient had to be measured exactly right. Each one added at just the right moment. The oven temperature had to be set precisely, and the timer for baking, what timer, Granny's eyes were sharper than any timer could ever be. She knew exactly when the crust was the perfect shade of golden brown, and just the right amount of elegant aroma filling the house, then, and only then, that the cake was ready to come out of the oven. Next came the icing. It was drizzled at just the exact time from the top to the bottom, appearing as though it was gliding down the slope of a beautiful mountain forming glistening snow. If drizzled when the cake was too hot, the icing would melt and not stay on the cake, and if it was too cool it would all clump up in one spot. My Granny had the process down to a science. Better yet, more than science, it was a work of art.

My Granny passed away in 2018, and though she left us with many precious memories, her pound cake is one I will treasure forever. Earlier that same year, something remarkable happened. For decades, people had asked her for the recipe, and she always refused. It was her secret. But one day, for reasons only she knew, she finally gave the coveted recipe to my dad. She sat him down, walked him through every step, and entrusted him with her prized creation. To this day, I don't know why she chose that moment, but my father got the elusive vanilla pound cake receipt. Since her passing, my dad has done his best to carry on the tradition. He makes her pound cake on special occasions, carefully following the recipe she gave him. And while his version is really good, often times mouthwatering, it's never quite the same as Granny. Each attempt gets him a little closer, but there's something about the way Granny did it that can't be replicated. Somehow, she had the touch.

Here's the thing, if you were to look at her recipe on paper, you'd probably notice it's not all that different from any other pound cake recipe. The ingredients include eggs, sugar, flour, butter, vanilla (and a few more no to be publicly revealed). But the true secret was in the attention to the details. Anyone can put ingredients together and bake them, but unless you follow Granny's instructions exactly, you'll never end up with her cake. The only way to get it right was to let her show you the path and trust her process.

That cake has become a representation, for me, of life itself. Each of us are traveling down our own path, trying to figure things out as we go. The question is this: are we using our own recipe, with our own shortcuts and substitutions, or are we following God's prefect recipe for our lives?

When we rely on ourselves, our recipe usually ends up full of a pound of pride and arrogance, a couple cups of selfishness and greed, and a few dashes of dishonesty, laziness, and envy. What do we do with those ingredients? We mix them together, throw them in the oven of life, and hope it comes out looking like success. More often than not, the end results are feelings of loss, hopelessness, and unsatisfaction.

But God's recipe is different. His ingredients and baking instructions call for trust in Him, several cups of His holy word, many ounces of patience, heaps of kindness and gentleness, sticks of faithfulness, and an endless supply of grace and love. When we take those ingredients and follow His directions, the end results are joy, peace, and a deep sense of faith. This path may not always be smooth or easy, but it leads to the life He created for us. An abundant life of comfort, security, purpose, and eternity in His care.

The Apostle Paul wrote in **Romans 8:28,** 28 And we know that in all things God works for the good of those who love Him, who have been called according to His purpose. Each ingredient God allows into our lives, whether sweet or bitter, enjoyable or painful, has a role to play in the greater recipe of life with Him. Some moments taste sour or flat on their own, but when combined with everything else under God's guidance, they become part of something beautiful, something prosperous, something complete.

Granny's pound cake was more than dessert. It was a reminder that perfection only comes when you trust the right recipe. And the greatest recipe of all isn't found in a kitchen, it's found in the Lord, guiding us step by step into the life He has prepared in advance for each of us.

"He guides me along the right path..."

By nature, sheep are creatures of habit. Without an external influence, a sheep will follow the same patterns of behavior day after day. Grazing, eating, wandering, and resting. Sheep will repeat their behaviors even to their own detriment and personal harm. Over grazing will desolate a plot of land turning it into a desert wasteland, while polluting the land and sources of water until they are infested with disease and parasites. Sheep will leave their own home and environment in complete ruin because of their lack of external awareness of their impact. Directing and leading of sheep is one of the most important responsibilities of the shepherd. A sheep's vision is limited. Their sense of direction is unreliable, and a sheep's awareness of threats of danger minimal. Without the shepherd's guidance, sickness, injury, and ultimately death is a sheep's fate.

This is why a shepherd's role to the flock is not simply to watch from a distance but to actively lead, often walking ahead to set the course. Sheep are disposed to take the path of least resistance, which is often straight into danger, scarcity, or exhaustion. Yet a good shepherd knows where the safe and nourishing paths are. The shepherd must know the way to fresh and clean water, safe and covered shelter, and land suitable for rest. Unlike a sheep left to its own devices, a shepherd is able to identify the places that may appear safe and lush, but lead to cliffs, predators, or dead ends. A good shepherd's guidance is not random or aimless. A good shepherd leads with purpose and intentionality. Their management is rooted in deep knowledge of the land and its terrain. They understand weather patterns, and soil compositions. They take responsibility and pride in recognizing and responding to situations and threats before the sheep have the slightest awareness of them. Under the care of a good shepherd, sheep can live a carefree life, grazing in the pasture, resting in the shade, drinking from clean pools of water and dew from lush grass. Completely unaware of the predators scared off, or the new patches of land prepped and prepared for grazing. The continued wellbeing of a sheep is determined by the path they take from pasture to pasture. A path can be self-determined, aimlessly taken into threats and desolation, or a path can be chosen that is led by the shepherd. The latter path is curated with purpose, knowledge, and intentionality for the comfort, security and welfare of the sheep.

For humans, our paths are not in reference to routes and roads we venture in life, but the spiritual and moral life-directions that guide our journeys. Similar to sheep, we too can venture on paths and journeys, and they will be either aimlessly following our own self compass and direction, or we can follow the path that the Good Shepherd intentionally and personally set before each of us. Human nature seems to gravitate to the easiest or most appealing routes at first glance; desiring shortcuts, smooth roads, and opportunities that garner quick results. But like most things in life, the easy way only leads to fleeting satisfaction, and superficial gratitude. The other option is taking the path lead by the Lord **Matthew 7:13-14** *13Enter through the narrow gate. For wide is the gate and broad is the road that leads to destruction, and many enter through it. 14 But small is the gate and narrow the road that leads to life, and only a few find it.*

Now, this path that is led by the Good Shepard, the Lord, will not be the smoothest. It will sometimes be a steep incline to test of our faith and endurance. Some journeys go through inclement weather that test our hope and perseverance. This path may lead us through shadowed valleys of pain and despair or make us feel alone on our voyage. Often times the path may cause to wonder if we should turnback to our previous paths, or a new path where we feel easy and comfort. Yet every turn, every incline, every pause along that road has a purpose. The "right path" will not always be the quickest, because our Good Shepherd is not guiding us based on convenience. The Good Shepherd wants so much more for our lives. The greatest benefit of following the Good Shepherd's path is that His path will always lead us closer to Him. In turn, closer proximity to our Lord comes with the tangible blessings of **protection, provision, prosperity**, and intangible virtues of **peace, joy, hope, and love**:

Protection
Psalms 91:1-16 1 Whoever dwells in the shelter of the Most High will rest in the shadow of the Almighty. 2 I will say of

the Lord, "He is my refuge and my fortress, my God, in whom I trust." 3 Surely he will save you from the fowler's snare and from the deadly pestilence. 4 He will cover you with his feather and under his wings you will find refuge; his faithfulness will be your shield and rampart. 5 You will not fear the terror of night, nor the arrow that flies by day, 6 nor the pestilence that stalks in the darkness, nor the plague that destroys at midday. 7 A thousand may fall at your side, ten thousand at your right hand, but it will not come near you. 8 You will only observe with your eyes and see the punishment of the wicked. 9 If you say, "The Lord is my refuge," and you make the Most High your dwelling, 10 no harm will overtake you; no disaster will come near your tent. 11 For he will command his angels concerning you to guard you in all your ways; 12 they will lift you up in their hands, so that you will not strike your foot against a stone. 13 You will tread on the lion and the cobra; you will trample the great lion and the serpent. 14 "Because he loves me," says the Lord, "I will rescue him; I will protect him, for he acknowledges my name. 15 He will call on me, and I will answer him; I will be with him in trouble, I will deliver him and honor him. 16 With long life I will satisfy him and show him my salvation."

Provision
Philippians 4:19 19 And my God will meet all your needs according to the riches of his glory in Christ Jesus.

Matthew 6:31-34 31 So do not worry, saying, 'What shall we eat?' or 'What shall we drink?' or 'What shall we wear?' 32 For the pagans run after all these things, and your heavenly Father knows that you need them. 33 But seek first his kingdom and his righteousness, and all these things will be given to you as well. 34 Therefore do not worry about tomorrow, for tomorrow will worry about itself. Each day has enough trouble of its own.

Prosperity
Psalms 5:12 12 Surely, Lord, you bless the righteous; you surround them with your favor as with a shield.

Proverbs 3:1-6 1 My son, do not forget my teaching, but keep my commands in your heart, 2 for they will prolong your life many years and bring you peace and prosperity. 3 Let love and faithfulness never leave you; bind them around your neck, write them on the tablet of your heart. Then you will win favor and a good name in the sight of God and man. 5 Trust in the Lord with all your heart and lean not on your own understanding; 6 in all your ways submit to him, and he will make your paths straight.

Peace
Numbers 6:24-26 24 "The Lord bless you and keep you; 25 the Lord make his face shine on you and be gracious to you; 26 the Lord turn his face toward you and give you peace.'"

John 14:25-27 25 "All this I have spoken while still with you. 26 But the Advocate, the Holy Spirit, whom the Father will send in my name, will teach you all things and will remind you of everything I have said to you. 27 Peace I leave with you; my peace I give you. I do not give to you as the world gives. Do not let your hearts be troubled and do not be afraid.

Joy
Psalms 16:8-11 8I keep my eyes always on the Lord. With him at my right hand, I will not be shaken. 9 Therefore my heart is glad and my tongue rejoices; my body also will rest

secure, ¹⁰ because you will not abandon me to the realm of the dead, nor will you let your faithful one see decay. ¹¹ You make known to me the path of life; you will fill me with joy in your presence, with eternal pleasures at your right hand.

Romans 15:13 ¹³May the God of hope fill you with all joy and peace as you trust in him, so that you may overflow with hope by the power of the Holy Spirit.

1 Peter 1:6-9 ⁶In all this you greatly rejoice though now for a little while you may have had to suffer grief in all kinds of trials. ⁷ These have come so that the proven genuineness of your faith, of greater worth than gold, which perishes even though refined by fire, may result in praise, glory and honor when Jesus Christ is revealed. ⁸ Though you have not seen him, you love him; and even though you do not see him now, you believe in him and are filled with an inexpressible and glorious joy, ⁹ for you are receiving the end result of your faith, the salvation of your souls.

Hope
Romans 15:13 ¹³May the God of hope fill you with all joy and peace as you trust in him, so that you may overflow with hope by the power of the Holy Spirit.

Psalms 31:21-24 ²¹ Praise be to the Lord, for he showed me the wonders of his love when I was in a city under siege. ²² In my alarm I said, "I am cut off from your sight!" Yet you heard my cry for mercy when I called to you for help. ²³ Love the Lord, all his faithful people! The Lord preserves those who are true to him, but the proud he pays back in full. ²⁴ Be strong and take heart, all you who hope in the Lord.

Love

Romans 5:1-5 ¹Therefore, since we have been
justified through faith, we have peace with God through our
Lord Jesus Christ, ² through whom we have gained access by
faith into this grace in which we now stand. And we boast in
the hope of the glory of God. ³ Not only so, but we also glory in
our sufferings, because we know that suffering produces
perseverance; ⁴ perseverance, character; and character,
hope. ⁵ And hope does not put us to shame, because God's
love has been poured out into our hearts through the Holy
Spirit, who has been given to us.

Romans 8:35–39 ³⁵Who shall separate us from the love of
Christ? Shall trouble or hardship or persecution or famine or
nakedness or danger or sword? ³⁶ As it is written: "For your
sake we face death all day long; we are considered as sheep to
be slaughtered." ³⁷ No, in all these things we are more than
conquerors through him who loved us. ³⁸ For I am convinced
that neither death nor life, neither angels nor demons, neither
the present nor the future, nor any powers, ³⁹ neither height
nor depth, nor anything else in all creation, will be able to
separate us from the love of God that is in Christ Jesus our
Lord.

1 John 3:1-3 ¹See what great love the Father has lavished on
us, that we should be called children of God! And that is what
we are! The reason the world does not know us is that it did
not know him. ² Dear friends, now we are children of God, and
what we will be has not yet been made known. But we know
that when Christ appears, we shall be like him, for we shall see

him as he is. 3 All who have this hope in him purify themselves, just as he is pure.

"...for His name's sake"

This brings us to the ladder portion in this section **for His name's sake**. The phrase "for His name's sake" reminds us of why He must lead the way in our lives. A shepherd's reputation is bound to the well-being of his flock. If the sheep are starving, injured, or lost it is a direct reflection on the shepherd's care. Likewise, God's guidance in our lives is tied to His character, and His name. He leads us along the right paths not only because He cares for us, absolutely love us, and desires for us to thrive and prosper with Him, but because this is His very nature and character. In the book of Exodus, we get an early account of God describing his very nature to Moses,

Exodus 34:5-7 5Then the Lord came down in the cloud and stood there with him and proclaimed his name, the Lord. 6 And he passed in front of Moses, proclaiming, "The Lord is compassionate and gracious God, slow to anger, abounding in love and faithfulness, 7maintaining love to thousands, and forgiving wickedness, rebellion and sin. We continue to see God's character and nature revealed throughout scripture:

Deuteronomy 32:3-4 3I will proclaim the name of the Lord. Oh, praise the greatness of our God! 4He is the Rock, his works are perfect, and all his ways are just. A faithful God who does no wrong, upright and just is he.

Psalms 103:2-10 2 Praise the Lord, my soul, and forget not all his benefits 3 who forgives all your sins and heals all your diseases, 4 who redeems your life from the pit and crowns you with love and compassion, 5 who satisfies your desires with good things so that your youth is renewed like the eagle's. 6 The Lord works righteousness and justice for all the oppressed. 7 He made known his ways to Moses, his deeds to the people of Israel: 8 The Lord is compassionate and gracious, slow to anger, abounding in love. 9 He will not always accuse, nor will he harbor his anger forever; 10 he does not treat us as our sins deserve or repay us according to our iniquities.

1 John 4:7-8 7Dear friends, let us love one another, for love comes from God. Everyone who loves has been born of God and knows God. 8 Whoever does not love does not know God, because God is love.

God does not guide us on our path out of obligation; He guides us out of love, with His integrity and character on the line. He does not need us, but we undoubtedly need Him to save us and continually lead us. We can trust His direction because His guidance is consistent with His unchanging nature. Our Good Shepherd's guidance is not simply about getting us to the next pasture; it is about shaping us to reflect His character throughout our journey and into eternity. Every step on the right path is an opportunity for His wisdom to correct us, His love to comfort us, and His faithfulness to be displayed through us.

Summary

"He guides me along the right paths for His name's sake" reminds us that God leads with intention, faithfulness, and knowledge that is revealed in His character, His name, and His word. Like sheep, on our own we are prone to wander and choose the easy and smooth paths of least resistance. However, with the guidance of the Good Shepherd we are led toward abundant life, and purpose with God. Though the path may not always be smooth, it always draws us closer to Him. The path of the Good Shepherd is never arbitrary; it is purposeful, personal, and marked by His wisdom and love. We can trust His path because it is consistent with who He is, a faithful, loving, and wise God. He does this for His name's sake, and our benefit, so that the world may see His compassion, His justice, His love and His glory manifested in us. The Good Shepherd's honor is bound to the care of His flock, and because God is unchanging, we can walk with confidence, knowing His path always leads to deliverance in the arms of the Good Shepherd. Our job is not to know every twist and turn ahead, but to simply stay close to Him, to trust and follow His voice, and to walk with Him in the confidence and the power God provides.

Ephesians 3:20 [20] Now to him who is able to do immeasurably more than we can ask or imagine

PART VII
Psalm 23 (NIV)

1 The Lord is my shepherd, I lack nothing.

2 He makes me lie down in green pastures, he leads me beside quiet waters,

3 he refreshes my soul. He guides me along the right paths for his name's sake.

4 **Even though I walk through the darkest valley, I will fear no evil, for you are with me**; your rod and your staff, they comfort me.

5 You prepare a table before me in the presence of my enemies. You anoint my head with oil; my cup overflows.

6 Surely your goodness and love will follow me all the days of my life, and I will dwell in the house of the Lord forever.

"Even though I walk through the darkest valley, I will fear no evil, for you are with me"

My Daughter's First Trip to the Doctor

Having children changed my whole perspective on love and what it means to care for another human being. Before my first child was born, I thought I understood love, but the first moment I held her changed my perception of love. I realized I would do anything for my daughter. The fatherly instincts kicked in immediately. With that instinct came a mindset that I would do everything in the power that God gave me to shield my daughter from any harm or pain.

When she turned two, my wife and I were scheduled to take her to the doctor for her annual checkup. Now, anyone who is blessed with children knows what that usually means, shots. This wasn't her first appointment with vaccinations, but it was the first time she was old enough to understand what getting shots meant. In prior wellness visits she didn't have the awareness to connect "the nurse with the needle" to the sting that followed. But now, at two years old, she had enough memory and imagination to dread what was coming.

Leading up to the appointment, my wife and I tried to prepare her. We told her why she needed to see the doctor, what the checkup would involve, and yes, that she had to get a couple of shots. The moment she heard the word "shots," her little face changed. Her smile faded, her body tensed, and I could almost see the memories flash through her mind. From then on, those shots became the center of all her questions: *"How big is the needle?", "Why do I have to get shots now?", "How many are they going to give me?", "Is it going to hurt a lot?"*

We did our best to answer each question gently and honestly. We tried to reassure her that it would be quick, and the shots were necessary to keep her healthy. We told her that we would be with her the whole time. Her little heart was filled with fear and worry. Nothing we said seemed to take those feelings away.

When the day of the appointment came, the battle began before we even left the house. She tried every trick in the book to escape. She would say things like:

"Daddy, my tummy hurts, I think I need to stay home and rest."

"Oh no! I left the lights on in the kitchen, we need to go back home!"

"Are you sure my appointment is today? Maybe it's tomorrow."

Her little excuses made me smile, but they also broke my heart. I could see how desperately she wanted to avoid what was coming. Still, my wife and I gently guided her into the car, reminding her we'd be with her every step of the way. At the doctor's office, everything started out fine. She handled the eyes, ears, nose, and lung checks without much a fuss. Then came the part she'd been dreading, the shots. I knelt down beside her as the nurse prepared the needles. I held her tiny hand in mine and looked into her beautiful wide eyes. *"Ok, honey,"* I said softly, *"remember what we talked about. Yes, it's going to hurt a little, but you don't have to be scared. I'll be right here with you. Just focus on me, it'll be over before you know it."* Her lip quivered, and with a trembling voice she said, *"Daddy, no. I don't want it. Don't let them hurt me."*

I swallowed hard, steadying myself as much as I was steadying her. *"Honey, they're not trying to hurt you, they're trying to help you."*

But she shook her head, tears starting to well up in her eyes. *"No, Daddy. They* are *going to hurt me, and you're letting them do it!"*

Those words cut me deeper than any needle ever could. To her, it looked like I was standing by while someone intentionally hurt her. My heart broke hearing the fear in her voice, but I tightened my grip on her little hand and whispered, *"Baby, I'm right here. I promise it will be ok. Daddy's not going anywhere."* She cried, she squirmed, and while the shots did hurt, she made it through. When it was over, the nurse handed her a sticker and a lollipop, and slowly her tears gave way to a proud little smile.

Walking out of that office, I realized something that my daughter couldn't yet understand. I knew those shots brought her pain, and I knew they scared her, but I also knew the purpose behind them. That temporary sting and pain was protecting her from far greater dangers she couldn't yet comprehend. At two years old, her world was too small to see the full picture. She only saw the needle and the hurt, not the sickness it would prevent or the health it would secure.

That day, I thought about how often we are forced to face our fears and how our heavenly father reacts. We look up at Him with tear-filled eyes, begging Him to stop the pain and wondering why He would let us go through something so hard. From our limited perspective, it can feel like He's just standing by, letting us suffer. But the truth is, He sees what we cannot see. He knows the bigger picture. He understands that sometimes the only way to protect us, to grow us, or to prepare us for what's ahead is to allow us to walk through temporary pain. It's not that He doesn't care. It's not that He doesn't hear our cries. The fact is, He loves us too much to trade long-term good for short-term comfort.

That doctor's visit became more than just a memory of my daughter's two-year checkup, it became a picture of faith, trust, and a Father's love that runs deeper than what we can see or imagine in the moment.

"Even though I walk through the darkest valley, I will fear no evil, for you are with me"

During David's time as a shepherd, he lived in the Judean hills around the town of Bethlehem. This metaphoric imagery of walking through the valley was actually an annual trip for him and his flock. With the changing of the season a journey was required to the high country where the sheep could graze in the lush mountain pastures. This was not a quick journey to the high country. Sheep take their time on their journey. They move slowly taking frequent stops to graze and eat along the way, gradually making their way up the hills as the snow melts away. Like every mountain trek, this is not an easy trip. Coincidentally just like life, the best and often quickest route to the top is always along the toughest path through treacherous valley terrain. Every mountain has its valley to venture through in order to reach the summit. These valleys are comprised of deep ravines, gorges, chasms and vast cliffs. The cliffs and rocks that rise on both sides can block out the light, creating long stretches of darkness. Hidden with that darkness, predators can be found lurking in the shadows. For a sheep, the valley is not just an inconvenience on their journey, but a place of fear.

The New International Version (NIV) bible uses the language "darkest valley", other translations describe this scenario as "valley of the shadow of death" – King James Version (KJV), "sunless valley of the shadow of death" – Amplified Bible (AMPC), "valley as dark as death" – Contemporary English Version (CEV). None of these translation sound like something one would want to experience in life, but just like the sheep we must go through these times in order to reach the mountain top. The top of the mountain is where we find luscious fresh green pastures and streams of crisp clear waters.

Similar to the danger associated with these journeys taken by the sheep are the valleys we face in our everyday lives. David writes, "***Even though*** I walk through the darkest valley..." not IF I walk through. Valleys are not a possibility in life; they are a certainty. These valleys come in a variety of scenarios, from the loss of loved ones, broken hearts, unachieved dreams, or tremendous disappointments and grief. It would be great to be able to just take a helicopter to the mountain top. Avoid all the pain and heartache, but God has a purpose for it all. Just as sheep must walk through the shadow filled paths; we too must walk through seasons where light seems absent and fear crouches close.

The apostles James wrote *2Consider it pure joy, my brothers and sisters, whenever you face trials of many kinds, 3 because you know that the testing of your faith produces perseverance. 4 Let perseverance finish its work so that you may be mature and complete, not lacking anything* (**James 1:2-4**). Without the trials we cannot appreciate the triumph. Whatever the situations, we must remember in order to move up, we must go through. And the best part of this section, "Even though I walk through the darkest valley, I will fear no evil, for **you are with me**".

Notice the change in tense from the earlier verses in Psalm 23. Up to this point, David has spoken of God in the third person: "He makes me lie down... He leads me... He restores my soul." But here, in the valley, David shifts to first and second tense: "You are with me." In the sunny, smooth, and pleasant pastures, the places of provision, peace and safety, it is enough to talk ABOUT God. However, in the darkest valleys, we must speak directly TO God. The Valleys of life move us from knowing about the Shepherd to calling on and clinging to the shepherd. It is an intimidate one-on-one relationship with the Lord.

The sheep, when walking in shadows of the valley, cannot see far ahead. Their vision is blocked and limited, but they do not need to see the path they are taking. If they stay close enough, they can hear the Shepherd's voice, and that is reassurance enough. His presence is their confidence. We have this same ability. We to can abide in His presence and discover our confidence in Him. For us, this truth is echoed throughout Scripture:

Isaiah 43:1-3 [1]But now, this is what the Lord says he who created you, Jacob, he who formed you, Israel: "Do not fear, for I have redeemed you; I have summoned you by name; you are mine. [2] When you pass through the waters, I will be with you; and when you pass through the rivers, they will not sweep over you. When you walk through the fire, you will not be burned; the flames will not set you ablaze. 3 For I am the Lord your God, the Holy One of Israel, your Savior;

Joshua 1:9 9Have I not commanded you? Be strong and courageous. Do not be afraid; do not be discouraged, for the Lord your God will be with you wherever you go.

Psalms 139:1-12 1You have searched me, Lord, and you know me. 2 You know when I sit and when I rise; you perceive my thoughts from afar. 3 You discern my going out and my lying down; you are familiar with all my ways. 4 Before a word is on my tongue you, Lord, know it completely. 5 You hem me in behind and before, and you lay your hand upon me. 6 Such knowledge is too wonderful for me, too lofty for me to attain. 7 Where can I go from your Spirit? Where can I flee from your presence? 8 If I go up to the heavens, you are there; if I make my bed in the depths, you are there. 9 If I rise on the wings of the dawn, if I settle on the far side of the sea, 10 even there your hand will guide me, your right hand will hold me fast. 11 If I say, "Surely the darkness will hide me and the light become night around me," 12 even the darkness will not be dark to you; the night will shine like the day, for darkness is as light to you.

The darkest valleys are where His presence becomes most treasured. We may not be delivered from the valley immediately, but we are sustained within it. We may not understand the reason for the valley, but we are never asked to walk it alone. The shadow of death, loss, or suffering can never fully overtake us because it is only a shadow. A shadow is powerless within light. The Good Shepherd Himself is our light, walking with us, ensuring that the darkness never has the final word.

Summary

"Even though I walk through the darkest valley, I will fear no evil, for you are with me" is not a promise of avoiding valleys, it is the assurance of God's presence in and through them. The valleys of life are unavoidable, but they are never unaccompanied. Valleys test us, press us, and sometimes terrify us, but they also teach us, mature us, and strengthen us. Even in the shadows of fear, loss, and uncertainty, the Good Shepherd's presence becomes our confidence, our courage, and our assurance. His voice is our guide. With Him beside us, the darkness loses its power, and we can keep walking forward in hope and faith until we reach the mountaintop. Indeed, the valley is not the end. The valley is the passage to a new destination of the knowledge of love and an experience of faith in the Lord. The Shepherd who leads us in and through will also lead us out.

PART VIII
Psalm 23

¹ The Lord is my shepherd, I lack nothing.

² He makes me lie down in green pastures, he leads me beside quiet waters,

³ he refreshes my soul. He guides me along the right paths for his name's sake.

⁴ Even though I walk through the darkest valley, I will fear no evil, for you are with me; **your rod and your staff, they comfort me**.

⁵ You prepare a table before me in the presence of my enemies. You anoint my head with oil; my cup overflows.

⁶ Surely your goodness and love will follow me all the days of my life, and I will dwell in the house of the Lord forever.

"your rod and your staff, they comfort me."

The walking stick and flashlight, they comfort me

Every summer, my family and I head out on a camping trip to Granby, Colorado. Granby is a small town tucked away in the middle of the Rocky Mountains, surrounded by some of the most breathtaking scenery in the state. Now, when I say camping, I don't mean the classic sense. There are no tents and lying down on the cold and hard uneven ground in sleeping bags. We do our camping in a yurt. Yurts are round wooden structures, covered with felt and insulated just enough to keep you from feeling completely exposed to the elements. They're simple, single-room lodgings, no running water, no heat or air conditioning, and no fancy amenities. Just four walls, a couple of bunk beds, two windows, and a door. It's one step down from glamping, and one step up from roughing it. The beauty of it is in its balance. It provides protection and the embraces of simplicity.

In the daytime, the temperature inside the yurt can soar past 100 degrees due to the insolation and lack of ventilation. But at night, once the sun dips behind the ridges, the temperature drops fast, often down into the single digits. That sudden shift in temperature has a way of humbling you. It reminds you quickly that you're a guest in the wilderness and are no longer in control.

Granby sits just south of Rocky Mountain National Park, which means wild animals are present and this is their natural dwelling place. It is the home of black bears, elks, moose, foxes, coyotes, and even silver wolves. While spotting one of these animals from a safe distance is thrilling, the possibility of running into one unexpectedly, especially at night, keeps you on your toes.

There is a separate bathhouse about a hundred yards uphill from the yurts. It sounds like no big deal until you're actually there, and it is nighttime, the fire has been put out, it is pitch black, the only light is the shining stars in the beautiful night sky. In these moments you realize that the family still needs to take the trek up the hill to brush their teeth and prepare for bed. That's when I reach for two things without fail: my walking stick and my flashlight. I never leave the yurt without those two things, and I mean never. If I even think about stepping outside without them, one of my kids will shout, *"dad, don't forget the stick and flashlight!"* Those two items have become more than tools during these trips. They're a kind of protection for us, a small layer of security in the vast uncertainty of the wilderness.

The walking stick is about protection and stability. It's six feet tall, strong, and solid. Something to lean on when the ground gets tricky, and something with a little power just in case we have an encounter with one of the many native animals of the area. Realistically, if I came face-to-face with a bear or a coyote, it's unlikely a stick would save the day, but it still feels protective. More important than physical protection, the stick provides some reassures and peace for my kids. They see me carrying it and they feel safer. That alone makes it worth dragging along.

As a matter of fact, on one particular trip the stick proved itself invaluable. Our trip is always booked well in advance, and in-between the booking and the actually trip I had a minor accident and tore my ACL. The trip was scheduled for two months post-surgery. Climbing the steep, rocky path to and from the bathhouse was no easy feat, but with the walking stick in hand, I had the stability that I needed. What started as a practical crutch since became a constant companion, a symbol of protection and steadiness in uncertain terrain.

Then there's the flashlight. And I'm not talking about a flimsy little keychain light. This is the real deal, the kind you see in late-night infomercials. This flashlight is blindingly bright with 50,000 lumens. It comes in a box with a bright red sticker on the side that reads "DO NOT LOOK DIRECTLY INTO LIGHT!" It cuts through the darkness like a sword, turning a shadowy, unknown trail into a visibly safe passage.

The path to the bathhouse is rugged. One wrong step could send you tumbling (I may or may not have rolled an ankle or two). This flashlight illuminates the way and provides visibility for each solid step. It's also my way of keeping the kids focused and close by my side. If one of them drifts too far off the path or gets distracted by something in the brush, a quick flash of the beam reels them back in. The light grabs their attention and refocuses their direction in its most literal sense.

Beyond their practical uses, the walking stick and flashlight are symbols for us. They represent protection & stability, and guidance & redirection. Together they give us comfort in the middle of the unknown. They are a reminder that even in the wilderness we have what we need to steady our steps and find our way forward. On those dark and cold nights in the Rocky Mountains when the sounds of the wild echo around us and the stars scatter across the sky, those two simple tools, the walking stick and the flashlight, become more than just gear. These tools are symbols of comfort, courage, and peace.

"Your rod and your staff, they comfort me"

For centuries, shepherds have been known to always possess two primary items when they are tending to their sheep, the rod and the staff. Though similar in look and form, these tools have distinct purposes that mutually work together to protect, guide, redirect and reassure the flock of their safety and prosperity. To most individuals, these items may seem very basic and ordinary; however, for sheep they symbolize order and peace. David, the shepherd, knew firsthand the invaluable necessity of each tool. In this Psalm, David paints a picture of His divine care through the use of these tools. When he affirms that "your rod and your staff, they comfort me," he is revealing how the Good Shepherd uses a metaphorical rod and staff to bring true comfort and peace to our lives. Let's examine these two tools and what they provide to us as God's sheep, grazing in the pastures of life.

The Rod: Protection and Authority

The rod is a strong and sturdy, club-like instrument, often crafted from the root of a tree. The rod symbolizes the shepherd's authority and strength. Its primary function is to protect. The rod can be used as a weapon against predators that threaten the shepherd's flock. In the wilderness, these threats come in the forms of wild animals and thieve. When the sheep are threatened, these threats are met with the full power and strength of the shepherd's rod. To the sheep the rod isn't a tool of harm rather an item of security and protection. Every time the rod is raised, it signals to the sheep that they are safe, and the shepherd will protect them.

In the same way, God's rod for us as His sheep is His holy word. His "rod" contains His promises and His power, readily available to reveals His faithfulness, His goodness, His love, and His desire to protect us from all harm. His word possesses authority and power over our threat the enemy. Scripture tells us that our adversary, the devil, roams like a roaring lion seeking whom he may devour (**1 Peter 5:8**). Our Good Shepherd does not leave us defenseless.

Hebrews 4:12 12 For the word of God is alive and active. Sharper than any double-edged sword, it penetrates even to dividing soul and spirit, joints and marrow; it judges the thoughts and attitudes of the heart.

Psalms 33:6-9 6 By the word of the Lord the heavens were made, their starry host by the breath of his mouth. 7 He gathers the waters of the sea into jars he puts the deep into storehouses. 8 Let all the earth fear the Lord; let all the people of the world revere him. 9 For he spoke, and it came to be; he commanded, and it stood firm.

Just as sheep draw comfort knowing their shepherd carries the rod, so we too can find comfort knowing our Good Shepherd and His Word stands between us and every threat. In the hands of most, a rod would just be a long stick or branch, but a shepherd has the power to draw out its purpose. In the shepherd's hand, the rod is not simply a stick of wood. It is carved by the shepherd with care and precision, weighted with strength, and carried as a sign of authority. To the sheep, it is a visual reminder that the shepherd is close. To lurking predators, it was a warning that danger would be met with force.

In the same way, God placed His Word in our lives as a rod of comfort. The holy scriptures carry His authority. Every command, every promise, every truth in the Word speaks with the weight of the Lord the Good Shepherd's voice. When doubts whisper or fears threaten to overwhelm us the Word of God stands like a rod, steady and unshaken, reminding us of who holds sovereign control.

The holy word is also our protection against the enemy. Temptations, lies, and the subtle pull of the world by the enemy are constant. By the "rod", God's word, loosen the enemies grip when confronted with the sharp double-edge sword of God's Word. Jesus resisted the enemy by speaking the Word, "It is written". We too can find safety when we hold to Scripture as our rod of defense. God's rod also has the authority for correction. At times, this correction is a gentle nudge that redirects us from straying too far. At other times, this correction is more firm drawing us back quickly to safety. Though correction can sting, it is never meant to harm. Correction is our Shepherd's way of keeping us safe, whole, and walking the right path. The rod is not a symbol of fear but of love and protection. The shepherd is always near, alert, and ready to protect. For us, the Word of God carries the same assurance. Each time we open God's holy word, we encounter His protection and care, and His power and authority.

The Staff: Guidance and Care
The perfect complement to the rod, is the staff. It is taller, more slender, and often has a crook on the end. It is not meant to be utilized as a weapon. It is an instrument of guidance and care. With the staff, the shepherd can gently nudge their sheep leading them onto safe paths, pull them

from dangerous situations, or draw them near for inspection and comfort. The staff embodies the personal relationship with the shepherd. It reminded the sheep that they are never forgotten, lost, or too far from the shepherd's reach.

The staff is a representation of the Holy Spirit in our lives. When we begin to wander and we step too close to the edge of sin or distraction, the gentle nudge of the Holy Spirit redirects us back to the Good Shepherd and his right path. Through God's Spirit, the Lord draws us close in a personal relationship that affirms He is God with us, Emmanuel. The Holy Spirit guides us in quiet ways, with inner promptings, stirrings of the heart, or whispers of truth that captures our attention and direct us onward when we're uncertain, confused, or led astray. When we fall into pits of shame, despair or discouragement, His "staff", the Holy Spirt reaches down to pull us back to the Good Shepherd our Lord. The rod speaks of strength; the staff speaks of tenderness.

John 16:13-15 13 But when he, the Spirit of truth, comes, he will guide you into all the truth. He will not speak on his own; he will speak only what he hears, and he will tell you what is yet to come. 14 He will glorify me because it is from me that he will receive what he will make known to you. 15 All that belongs to the Father is mine. That is why I said the Spirit will receive from me what he will make known to you."

John 14:26-27 26 But the Advocate, the Holy Spirit, whom the Father will send in my name, will teach you all things and will remind you of everything I have said to you. 27 Peace I leave with you; my peace I give you. I do not give to you as the world gives. Do not let your hearts be troubled and do not be afraid.

Isaiah 30:21 21Whether you turn to the right or to the left, your ears will hear a voice behind you, saying, "This is the way; walk in it."

Exodus 15:1-13 1"I will sing to the Lord, for he is highly exalted. Both horse and driver he has hurled into the sea. 2 "The Lord is my strength and my defense; he has become my salvation. He is my God, and I will praise him, my father's God, and I will exalt him. 3 The Lord is a warrior; the Lord is his name. 4 Pharaoh's chariots and his army he has hurled into the sea. Pharaoh's officers are drowned in the Red Sea. 5 The deep waters have covered them; they sank to the depths like a stone. 6 Your right hand, Lord, was majestic in power. Your right hand, Lord, shattered the enemy. 7 "In the greatness of your majesty you threw down those who opposed you. You unleashed your burning anger; it consumed them like stubble. 8 By the blast of your nostrils the waters piled up. The surging waters stood up like a wall; the deep waters congealed in the heart of the sea. 9 The enemy boasted, I will pursue, I will overtake them. I will divide the spoils; I will gorge myself on them. I will draw my sword, and my hand will destroy them.10 But you blew with your breath, and the sea covered them. They sank like lead in the mighty waters. 11 Who among the gods is like you, Lord? Who is like you, majestic in holiness, awesome in glory, working wonders? 12 "You stretch out your right hand, and the earth swallows your enemies. 13 In your unfailing love you will lead the people you have redeemed. In your strength you will guide them to your holy dwelling.

Psalm 34:15-20 15 The eyes of the Lord are on the righteous, and his ears are attentive to their cry; 16 but the face of

the Lord is against those who do evil, to blot out their
name from the earth. [17] The righteous cry out, and
the Lord hears them; he delivers them from all their troubles.
[18] The Lord is close to the brokenhearted and saves those who
are crushed in spirit. [19] The righteous person may have many
troubles, but the Lord delivers him from them all; [20] he
protects all his bones, not one of them will be broken.

Summary

If the rod is the shepherd's tool of authority, the staff is his
tool of care. Together, they remind us that God is our
Protector and our Guide. Where the rod carried strength, the
staff carried gentleness. The rod and the staff paint a picture
of the Shepherd's care. His Word stands as authority,
strength, and protection. His Spirit guides with nearness,
tenderness, and rescue. One protects us from the external
dangers while the other helps us with the internal weaknesses
and struggles. The sheep found comfort not in one tool alone,
but in the combination of both. Without the rod, the sheep
would be unprotected, yet without the staff, they would be
lost. But together, the two create the perfect balance, and this
balance is essential for peace and comfort with our Good
Shepherd.

We can find comfort in knowing our Shepherd is strong
enough to defeat all our adversaries, and tender enough to
guide us when we falter. His authority and His intimacy work
hand in hand. The same God who commands armies of angels
also bends low to carry us when we are weak.

"Your rod and your staff, they comfort me." This declaration reveals that God's comfort is not passive but active, not distant but present. Just as a shepherd uses both tools daily in the pasture, so our Lord uses His Word and His Spirit daily in our lives.

- The **rod,** God's word, assures us of His protection and power.
- The **staff,** the Holy Spirit, assures us of His presence and guidance.
- **Together**, they assure us of Emmanuel, God with us.

The comfort of the Good Shepherd is not found in the absence of danger or difficulty, but in the certainty of His presence and care. When enemies rise, His rod defends us. When we stray, His staff restores us. When we fear, His tools remind us: We are His, and He will not leave us nor forsake us.

So, like sheep in the pasture, we can rest. We may walk through valleys, face shadows of physical and spiritual darkness, and endure trials, but by knowing that our Good Shepherd carries both a rod and a staff we can find peace. The rod and the staff stand together as symbols of the Shepherd's complete care. The **rod**, firm and strong, pointing us to the power and authority of God's Word, defending against danger, exposing lies, and correcting us when we wander. The **staff**, gentle and steady, reflecting the Holy Spirit, guiding us in truth, drawing us close, and rescuing us when we fall.

Together, they remind us that God's care is never one-dimensional. He is both protector and guide, defender and comforter. His Word sets our foundation, while His Holy

Spirit walks with us daily. To know the Good Shepherd is to rest in him: the power of His wisdom and the presence of His Holy Spirit.

PART IX
Psalm 23

¹ The Lord is my shepherd, I lack nothing.

² He makes me lie down in green pastures, he leads me beside quiet waters,

³ he refreshes my soul. He guides me along the right paths for his name's sake.

⁴ Even though I walk through the darkest valley, I will fear no evil, for you are with me; your rod and your staff, they comfort me.

⁵ **You prepare a table before me in the presence of my enemies**. You anoint my head with oil; my cup overflows.

⁶ Surely your goodness and love will follow me all the days of my life, and I will dwell in the house of the Lord forever.

"You prepare a table before me in the presence of my enemies."

Setting the table of life

For anyone who has ever truly prepared a table for a meal, they know it's no small task. It takes attention, effort, detail, and a kind of care that often goes unnoticed. The irony is that the people who sit down at that table to eat the meal rarely realize just how much time and effort went into making it beautiful, well before they ever stepped to the table. We just sit down, eat a phenomenally prepared meal, and go about our evening.

When I was growing up, my family only ate at a fully prepared table twice a year, Thanksgiving and Christmas. These were special celebration meals, the ones where extended family crowded into the house, laughter filled the rooms, and the aroma of turkey, ham, macaroni and cheese and sweet potato pies drifted out of the kitchen hours before we even sat down. My mom would go all out, not just with the food but with the dining room itself. We knew it was special because the dining room wasn't a room we used every day. In fact, those two holidays were the only time we were even allowed to step foot in there.

As a young kid, I never thought much about what went into getting that table set. Although I didn't notice it, my mom was up early in the morning getting everything ready for the special day. When nighttime arrived, the meal just appeared, and all I knew was that the dining room suddenly transformed into a place fit for royalty. But when I got older, my mom started asking me and my brother to help with the preparations. The first time she asked me to help set the table was when I learned the truth. Preparing a table was no small feat, it was work, serious work. It always started with the tablecloth.

"T, can you grab the tablecloth and get it ready please?" she'd call from the kitchen.

"Sure thing, Mom," I'd reply, grabbing the tablecloth from the linen closet. It was massive, about nine feet long and six feet wide. I unfolded it, spread it across the table, and smoothed it with my hands, and before she knew it, I was back in my room watching TV.

"T, come back down here. What is this? She said, *"You need to iron it first." "Iron the tablecloth?"* I'd repeat, baffled. To me, it was just going to get covered in plates and food anyway.

"Yes," she said firmly, *"iron it please."*

So, I hauled the massive tablecloth over to the ironing board. Thirty minutes later, I was still sweating over what felt like an endless sea of fabric, battling deep creases from being folded up in the closet for months. Finally, I draped the now smooth cloth across the table, proud of my work.

Before I could step back, I heard my mom's voice again, *"No-no, you need to wipe down the table first."*

"Wipe down a table that's about to get covered by a tablecloth?" I asked, genuinely confused.

My mom replied, *"Boy, just wipe it down and stop asking so many questions."*

"Got it mom."

Once the table was wiped and covered, I went to the kitchen for plates. I stacked a few in my arms and headed toward the dining room when my mom stopped me mid-step and asked

"What are you doing?"

"Getting the plates for the table," I said.

"What about the seat back covers?" she questioned.

"Seat back covers? We have seat back covers?"

"Yes!" she shot back. *"They're in the linen closet under the tablecloths."*

Sure enough, there they were. I had never noticed them before. And of course, they needed ironing too. Another thirty or forty minutes later, every chair had a crisp and perfect cover. Finally, it was time for the place settings. As I reached for the plates she says:

"Don't forget the placemats".

"Yes, ma'am" I reply.

By this point, I thought I had finally made some progress. Tablecloth, seat covers, placemats, plates. Next had to be the utensils.

"Did you grab the salad plates", I heard from the other room.

At this point I figured I would just ask all I needed to put out before I did it wrong and needed to redo it. So, I asked

"Mom, what all do I need to put out with the plates?"

She replied, *"You will need the salad plates, salad and dinner forks, dinner knifes, spoons, water glasses, wine glasses, dessert forks, and a napkin for each place setting."*

"And I bet they all need to go in a certain spot, right?", I asked, while slumping my shoulders in disappointment just from hearing it all.

"Yes, T," she answered with that look only moms can give.

So, I placed each one carefully in its correct place. Forks on the left, knives and spoons on the right, and napkins folded into those fancy triangles she liked. I was proud of my work. I thought I was finished. I even started to walk toward the couch, ready to collapse into it and watch some football. But then I heard her soft voice again.

"What about the rest of the table?"

The rest? I thought. I already did all the place settings. I even folded the napkins nice.

She continued, *"You still need the candles, the centerpiece, the salt and pepper. And did you rinse the wine and water glasses before you put them on the table?"*

Two hours later, the table was finally complete.

What I thought would be a quick, easy task turned into a full morning event, and even more importantly a life lesson. Every detail mattered. Every wrinkle smoothed, every glass polished, every piece in its proper place, it all came together to create the kind of table that welcomed family and made holidays feel like more than just another day. Only then did I begin to realize the weight of what my mom had been doing all those years. She wasn't just setting a table. She was creating an atmosphere. She was building a memory. She was showing us, in her own way, the kind of love that goes into preparation long before anyone else even arrives to sit down.

"You prepare a table before me" hits differently when you've taken the time to set a table yourself. When God "prepares a table before us" He irons the tablecloth of our lives, straightening each detail, He sets every plate and utensil in its proper place, not halfway, not rushed, but with thought and care. He does not set the table in secret or in safety, but right in the middle of life's chaos, in the presence of those who oppose us, in the very places where we feel most vulnerable.

Just like my mom, who prepared that table long before the guests ever walked through the door, God is already at work preparing what we will need before we arrive. Often times we don't even realize the preparation and effort that was planned for us. The table was set and the meal prepared. We just showed up in the dining room, pulled up a chair, and ate a blessed meal. The Lord is constantly setting a table to feed us. This is not a physical feeding, but a feeding of His presence, His love, and His word. His daily bread is carefully woven into every detail of our lives.

In this Psalm, David was not referring to what we traditionally think of when we speak of a table or a piece of furniture. For sheep, the notion of a "table" referred to pastures that were grazed by the sheep during the summer months. These pastures were often in the flat lands or plateaus of the mountains. These plateaus were flat-top lands that were not naturally ready for grazing; they had to be prepped and prepared for the flock well in advance by the shepherd. The shepherd would need to ensure the vegetation was adequate for eating by removing poisonous plants and make sure that clean water sources were available for drinking. The shepherd needed to survey the terrain to guarantee it was safe for grazing by removing unnecessary rocks, and filling holes to prevent its sheep from falling or getting cast down. The final stage for preparation that was required was the shepherd needed to drive out any predators from the pasture. Only after this preparation could the sheep enter the land to eat, to drink, to graze, and to rest in a land that was safe and nutritious. By the time the sheep arrived at the tableland, the shepherd's diligent and immense efforts of preparations, turned a place of potential dangers into a land of peace and comfort. Every need and desire of the sheep was thoughtfully prepared and provided.

Just as the shepherd works diligently to prepare a "table" for his sheep, our Good Shepherd the Lord does the same for us. God is working and preparing for our comfort and well-being and peace before we step into each season of life. Whether it be a new job, a move to a new city, or even as simple as a drive down the highway, the Lord is always preparing a path. His care for us is proactive, not reactive. We see this idea of prepared provision by God to His people throughout the Bible:

Isaiah 45:2-3 [2] I will go before you and will level the mountains; I will break down gates of bronze and cut through bars of iron. [3] I will give you hidden treasures, riches stored in secret places, so that you may know that I am the Lord, the God of Israel, who summons you by name.

Exodus 23:20 [20] "See, I am sending an angel ahead of you to guard you along the way and to bring you to the place I have prepared.

Deuteronomy 1:29-31 [29] Then I said to you, "Do not be terrified; do not be afraid of them. [30] The Lord your God, who is going before you, will fight for you, as he did for you in Egypt, before your very eyes, [31] and in the wilderness. There you saw how the Lord your God carried you, as a father carries his son, all the way you went until you reached this place."

Philippians 4:6-7 [6] Do not be anxious about anything, but in every situation, by prayer and petition, with thanksgiving, present your requests to God. [7] And the peace of God, which transcends all understanding, will guard your hearts and your minds in Christ Jesus.

We never arrive at a table by chance. Under the Good. Shepherd's care, we are brought to a place that the Good Shepherd has already walked. The places that we fear to enter such as that job interview, that tough conversation, or that relocation to a new place, the Lord has already walked through the place and prepared it just for us. When we arrive at circumstances that feel hostile or uncertain, we must trust that our Good Shepherd has already been there, and the table has already been set for us. We just need to sit down in His securely and love. The table has already been set for us to eat and prosper.

"...in the presence of my enemies"

During the time that the shepherd is preparing the land for its flock, they drive out all potential predators from the grazing land. The shepherd does not remove threats from the entire landscape. The sheep graze on the manicured land while predators watch from a distance. The shepherd is always vigilant and ready to protect the sheep and fend off any enemy. In this way, predators are forced to watch sheep thrive and prosper under the watchful care of the shepherd. It is the same for us as followers of our Good Shepherd the Lord.

God does not promise a life without adversity and opposition. He promises a life of provision and protection in the midst of our enemies. Enemies such as fear, doubt, sickness, pain, death, betrayal, even individuals who wish us harm may surround us; however, we are under the watchful eye and care of the Good Shepherd. The Lord, our Good Shepherd, is ready and willing, with his rod and staff, to step in and protect us. Our enemies are powerless to prevent our Good Shepherd from tending and sustaining us. His peace and comfort are available for those that will follow Him to the table that has been prepared specifically for each of us. Here we see a few stories of the Good Sheperd preparing the table in the midst of enemies, and His provisions and protection overcoming all.

Daniel dined at such a table in the lion's din:

Daniel 6:16-27 16 So the king gave the order, and they brought Daniel and threw him into the lions' den. The king said to Daniel, "May your God, whom you serve continually, rescue you!" 17 A stone was brought and placed over the mouth of the den, and the king sealed it with his own signet ring and with the rings of his nobles, so that Daniel's situation might not be changed. 18 Then the king returned to his palace and spent the night without eating and without any entertainment being brought to him. And he could not sleep. 19 At the first light of dawn, the king got up and hurried to the lions' den. 20 When he came near the den, he called to Daniel in an anguished voice, "Daniel, servant of the living God, has your God, whom you serve continually, been able to rescue you from the lions?" 21 Daniel answered, "May the king live forever! 22 My God sent his angel, and he shut the mouths of the lions. They have not hurt me, because I was found innocent in his sight. Nor have I ever done any wrong before you, Your Majesty." 23 The king was overjoyed and gave orders to lift Daniel out of the den. And when Daniel was lifted from the den, no wound was found on him, because he had trusted in his God. 24 At the king's command, the men who had falsely accused Daniel were brought in and thrown into the lions' den, along with their wives and children. And before they reached the floor of the den, the lions overpowered them and crushed all their bones. 25 Then King Darius wrote to all the nations and peoples of every language in all the earth: "May you prosper greatly! 26 "I issue a decree that in every part of my kingdom people must fear and reverence the God of Daniel. "For he is the living God and he endures forever; his kingdom will not be destroyed, his dominion will never end. 27 He rescues and he saves; he performs signs and wonders in the heavens and on the earth. He has rescued Daniel from the power of the lions."

Three Hebrew boys Shadrach, Meshach and Abendego:
Daniel 3:16-28 16 Shadrach, Meshach and Abednego replied to him, "King Nebuchadnezzar, we do not need to defend ourselves before you in this matter. 17 If we are thrown into the blazing furnace, the God we serve is able to deliver us from it, and he will deliver us from Your Majesty's hand. 18 But even if he does not, we want you to know, Your Majesty, that we will not serve your gods or worship the image of gold you have set up." 19 Then Nebuchadnezzar was furious with Shadrach, Meshach and Abednego, and his attitude toward them changed. He ordered the furnace heated seven times hotter than usual 20 and commanded some of the strongest soldiers in his army to tie up Shadrach, Meshach and Abednego and throw them into the blazing furnace. 21 So these men, wearing their robes, trousers, turbans and other clothes, were bound and thrown into the blazing furnace. 22 The king's command was so urgent and the furnace so hot that the flames of the fire killed the soldiers who took up Shadrach, Meshach and Abednego, 23 and these three men, firmly tied, fell into the blazing furnace. 24 Then King Nebuchadnezzar leaped to his feet in amazement and asked his advisers, "Weren't there three men that we tied up and threw into the fire?" They replied, "Certainly, Your Majesty." 25 He said, "Look! I see four men walking around in the fire, unbound and unharmed, and the fourth looks like a son of the gods." 26 Nebuchadnezzar then approached the opening of the blazing furnace and shouted, "Shadrach, Meshach and Abednego, servants of the Most High God, come out! Come here!" So, Shadrach, Meshach and Abednego came out of the fire, 27 and the satraps, prefects, governors and royal advisers crowded

around them. They saw that the fire had not harmed their bodies, nor was a hair of their heads singed; their robes were not scorched, and there was no smell of fire on them. 28 Then Nebuchadnezzar said, "Praise be to the God of Shadrach, Meshach and Abednego, who has sent his angel and rescued his servants! They trusted in him and defied the king's command and were willing to give up their lives rather than serve or worship any god except their own God.

Elijah ate at such a table when ravens fed him in the wilderness
1Kings 17:1-6 1 Now Elijah the Tishbite, from Tishbe in Gilead, said to Ahab, "As the Lord, the God of Israel, lives, whom I serve, there will be neither dew nor rain in the next few years except at my word." 2 Then the word of the Lord came to Elijah: 3 "Leave here, turn eastward and hide in the Kerith Ravine, east of the Jordan. 4 You will drink from the brook, and I have directed the ravens to supply you with food there." 5 So he did what the Lord had told him. He went to the Kerith Ravine, east of the Jordan, and stayed there. 6 The ravens brought him bread and meat in the morning and bread and meat in the evening, and he drank from the brook.

The enemies in the above real-life stories were liars, killers, and idolaters that were nearby watching the people of God, but they could not prevent the Lord from taking care of His people. The same is true for us today. Our enemy, Satan, comes to steal our identity, kill our purpose, and destroy our relationships. Yet still, our Good Shepherd has prepared a table for us, and none of the enemy cannot stop the Good Shepherd from protecting and providing for His flock.

Summary

"You prepare a table before me in the presence of my enemies" is not a promise of a life without struggle, but a declaration of God's care within the struggle. The image of the prepared table reminds us that God's care is not only about survival but about an abundant life now and yet to come. He does not lead us to barren places with just enough to scrape by. Instead, He spreads a feast in the very places we once feared. The presence of our enemies does not cancel His provision for us; in fact, it highlights it. What was meant to intimidate us becomes the backdrop to experience His generosity.

This verse shifts our focus from what surrounds us to who sustains us. Enemies may remain for a little while, but they are powerless in the presence of the Good Shepherd. His preparation goes before us, His protection surrounds us, and His peace steadies us.

In the end, the table is more than provision; it is a testimony of the goodness and greatness of what God planned for us. Every time we eat the daily bread that He has prepared, we declare that our Good Shepherd is greater than any enemy. Greater than any fear, threat, doubt, or opposition. His goodness does not just follow us into safe pastures; it goes before us and prepares the place for our arrival. The work is already done, it is on us to sit and eat, trust and obey our Good Shepherd. The Lord is always present, and with him we thrive in His peace.

PART X
Psalm 23

¹ The Lord is my shepherd, I lack nothing.

² He makes me lie down in green pastures, he leads me beside quiet waters,

³ he refreshes my soul. He guides me along the right paths for his name's sake.

⁴ Even though I walk through the darkest valley, I will fear no evil, for you are with me; your rod and your staff, they comfort me.

⁵ You prepare a table before me in the presence of my enemies. **You anoint my head with oil**; my cup overflows.

⁶ Surely your goodness and love will follow me all the days of my life, and I will dwell in the house of the Lord forever.

"You anoint my head with oil"

Saturday Morning Cartoons and the Anointing

When I was growing up, Saturday mornings were sacred times for me as a kid. "Saturday Morning Cartoons" was a consistent event for my brother and me. We looked forward to Saturday mornings all week long. We enjoyed everything that we watched on Saturday mornings, but one cartoon in particular stood above the rest, The X-Men. The moment that guitar riff hit, the one every 90s kid can hum by heart, we were glued to the TV. For that half hour, our living room wasn't just a living room; it was a world of heroes and villains, moral tension, and high-stakes battles. It wasn't just something to watch. It was an epic adventure.

Every character had their moment of glory, but for me, Wolverine was the greatest character. He was the mean and strong, had super healing factor, and no other hero could beat that. Despite those facts, my brother's favorite character was Magneto. Some would categorize Magneto as the head antagonist or villain on the TV series. As a kid, I could not figure out how a villain could be his favorite character. But looking back now, I realize why he stood out to him. Magneto wasn't just powerful; he was the most complex and compelling figure of all the X-Men characters. He was complicated, opposing viewpoints to the X-men, yet sometimes he was an ally. Born Erik Lehnsherr, he is a survivor of the Holocaust. A man shaped by trauma and persecution, who believes that mutants must fight to prevent the same kind of suffering he, his family, and community once endured. Magneto's life struggles drove him to extremism. He carried his trauma like armor, and it shaped how he saw the world. What made Magneto memorable, though, wasn't only his power but his conviction that mutants must fight, "by any means necessary" for their right. He wasn't your typical antagonist or villain.

My brother and I would go back and forth about who was the strongest or would win in a fight. Even though Wolverine was my pick, I did have to admit that Magneto possessed the best mutant powers. He had the ability to control magnetic fields, which meant he could manipulate metal, generate powerful force fields, and even fly by controlling the Earth's magnetic pull. Even his helmet held superpower. It was one of his defining symbols, sleek, angular, and always slightly menacing. Beyond its striking look, the helmet served a critical purpose: it blocked telepathic attacks, particularly from his arch nemesis Professor Xavier. The helmet allowed him to keep his thoughts his own, no one could read his mind, influence him, or make him doubt his mission. It was a covering and protection from intrusive thoughts and distractions. Under that covering, Magneto was untouchable, his convictions guarded, his purpose undisturbed.

There's a strange comfort in that image. Because in life, our minds, full of thoughts and reasoning, are continually under spiritual attack. Through the avenues of television, social media, music, false teachings, and other people, our minds are constantly being bombarded. This informational junk can lead to fear, anxiety, doubt, hopelessness, and unbelief. These external voices and subliminal messages can distort what God has already spoken over us. Like Magneto's helmet, this Psalm speaks to a covering and protection. God provides us with his own supernatural helmet of covering and protection.

"You anoint my head with oil"

Shepherds, to this day, rely on oil as a critical measure of caring for their sheep. Especially during the summer months. Swarms of insects and particularly flies are rampant in the pastures. If allowed, these flies, nasal flies in particular, can be a sheep's greatest tormentors. Sheep are most vulnerable around the head and nose region, and these flies will buzz around the sheep's head attempting to lay their eggs in the moist mucous of their nose. If they are successful in their task, in just a few days, these eggs will hatch into larva in the nose. These larvae will work their way up the nasal passage and into the sheep's head. Once they are deep inside the sheep's head, these larvae will cause extreme irritation and pain. The sheep will begin to display desperate action to obtain any form of relief from this agonizing annoyance. They will intentionally bash their heads against trees, rocks, fence posts, or brushes. In severe cases, a sheep may end up killing itself in a frantic panic to find peace from this torment.

The simple presence of flies and other insect swarms, sheep will become visually restless, anxious, and fearful. They will begin to display erratic behaviors in their attempt to escape these tormentors. They stamp their feet erratically, pacing from place to place around the pasture, or even hiding and refusing to graze. All these harmful behaviors are desperate attempts to escape from these attacks. These tormentors can ultimately eliminate all comfort and peace within the flock.

Applying oil over the sheep's head, nose, eyes, and ears has been an effective protective measure and remedy of relief for sheep from these tormenters. By covering a sheep's head and fleece with oil, it would repel the onslaught of insect, and most importantly, prevent nasal flies from landing on the sheep nasal passage and laying eggs. If a sheep is already in distress due to these insects, the shepherd's oil will bring the sheep instant relief. It sooths the skin, heals the cuts, and acts as a barrier against pests and disease. Promptly upon application a clear change in behavior can be noticed. The shepherd's oil is both a peacekeeper and peace provider in the mist of attacks and agitations.

Drawing from his firsthand experience as a shepherd, David, illuminates how God is keenly aware of the needs of His people. God tenderly cares for us with both proactive measures to prevent harm and retroactive measure to relieve our afflictions. When David declared, "You (God) anoint my head with oil," he was revealing to us that the Good Shepherd ministers to the areas of our greatest weakness and need. Just as the shepherd applies oil where the sheep are most vulnerable, so the Lord applies His presence, His grace, and His healing where our hearts are most vulnerable and fragile.

Oftentimes we face our own "swarms of flies" that attempt to infiltrate our mind and heart. These "flies" constantly attack us by trying to rob us of the love and the peace our Good Shepherd desires to provide us. Worry, temptation, and fear, constantly swirling around us. Social media, television, news outlets, negative friends, and gossips spewing coworkers, can all distort the truth and reality that God intends for us. The constant noise and disruptions from the world can burrow into our thoughts like spiritual parasites. Left unchecked, these things steal our peace, distract our focus, and lead us into harmful ungodly patterns of behavior. We can become sheep, looking for any relieve possible if left unchecked.

There is only one answer to these daily torments, and that is
the Good Shepherd's oil, God's anointing. By His Spirit,
pouring in us and upon us, He guards our minds and
regenerates our hearts. His truth repels the lies of the enemy,
His peace quiets the anxious thoughts of the world, and His
presence brings rest. Just as the oil provides the relief needed
for the sheep to find peace and rest, the Holy Spirit keeps us
from being consumed by destructive thoughts and patterns.
His anointing is not only for great battles or moments of
triumph; it is a quiet daily defense of our souls against the
relentless attempts of the enemy to control are minds and
behaviors.

The Oil: Healing and Renewal
The shepherd's oil is practical care for sheep, and in Scripture,
oil also carries deep spiritual meaning of an anointing. It
symbolizes consecration, favor, and the work of the Holy
Spirit. To be anointed by God is to be set apart, strengthened,
and supplied with His divine presence for his divine purpose.

1 Samuel 16:1…7- 13 [1] The Lord said to Samuel, "How long
will you mourn for Saul, since I have rejected him as king over
Israel? Fill your horn with oil and be on your way; I am
sending you to Jesse of Bethlehem. I have chosen one of his
sons to be king."

[7] But the Lord said to Samuel, "Do not consider his appearance
or his height, for I have rejected him. The Lord does not look
at the things people look at. People look at the outward
appearance, but the Lord looks at the heart…" [10] Jesse had
seven of his sons pass before Samuel, but Samuel said to him,
"The Lord has not chosen these." [11] So he asked Jesse, "Are
these all the sons you have?" "There is still the youngest,"

Jesse answered. "He is tending the sheep." Samuel said, "Send for him; we will not sit down until he arrives." 12 So he sent for him and had him brought in. He was glowing with health and had a fine appearance and handsome features. Then the Lord said, "Rise and anoint him; this is the one." 13 So Samuel took the horn of oil and anointed him in the presence of his brothers, and from that day on the Spirit of the Lord came powerfully upon David. Samuel then went to Ramah.

Psalms 92:5-11 5How great are your works, Lord, how profound your thoughts! 6 Senseless people do not know, fools do not understand, 7 that though the wicked spring up like grass and all evildoers flourish, they will be destroyed forever. 8 But you, Lord, are forever exalted. 9 For surely your enemies, Lord, surely your enemies will perish; all evildoers will be scattered. 10 You have exalted my horn like that of a wild ox; fine oils have been poured on me. 11 My eyes have seen the defeat of my adversaries; my ears have heard the rout of my wicked foes.

Romans 15:13 13 May the God of hope fill you with all joy and peace as you trust in him, so that you may overflow with hope by the power of the Holy Spirit.

2 Corinthians 3:17-18 17 Now the Lord is the Spirit, and where the Spirit of the Lord is, there is freedom. 18 And we all, who with unveiled faces contemplate the Lord's glory, are being transformed into his image with ever-increasing glory, which comes from the Lord, who is the Spirit.

Isaiah 61:1 1The Spirit of the Sovereign Lord is on me, because the Lord has anointed me to proclaim good news to the poor. He has sent me to bind up the brokenhearted, to proclaim freedom for the captives and release from darkness for the prisoners

John 14:23-27 23 Jesus replied, "Anyone who loves me will obey my teaching. My Father will love them, and we will come to them and make our home with them. 24 Anyone who does not love me will not obey my teaching. These words you hear are not my own; they belong to the Father who sent me. 25 "All this I have spoken while still with you. 26 But the Advocate, the Holy Spirit, whom the Father will send in my name, will teach you all things and will remind you of everything I have said to you. 27 Peace I leave with you; my peace I give you. I do not give to you as the world gives. Do not let your hearts be troubled and do not be afraid.

In our daily lives, God's anointing is his healing touch that cover us. It protects us from harm and soothes our wounds, our hurts and our pains. These hurts and pains can be both visible and those only God can see. It is this divine protection that keeps our minds at peace when negative or unwanted feelings press upon us. It is the renewing grace that strengthens us when our souls are weary. When the distractions of the flesh, the desires of the world, and the enemy is at work in our lives, the Good Shepherd's Spirit applies His oil of truth (if we are willing to obey). When sin infects us, God's mercy redeems. When despair distract us the Father's love restores.

Summary

"You anoint my head with oil" is more than a picture of comfort, it is a promise of God's attentiveness to our thoughts, our situations, our behaviors, and our pain. It is a confirmation of His nearness to us in our daily lives. Just as a shepherd applied oil with his own hands during David's time, our Good Shepherd personally anoints each one of us with His Spirit to live in his will. This anointing protects us from what would destroy our peace, heals the wounds we cannot mend on our own, and points us to the truth about God's sovereignty in our lives.

The shepherd did not wait until his sheep were injured beyond repair; he applied the oil daily as prevention and protection. In the same way, God works in our lives to guard us before harm takes root, and to heal what is broken. He gives us discernment through His Spirit, conviction through His Word, and the peace of His presence to keep us firm with him when life presses in.

When our Good Shepherd anoints our heads with His oil, we are protected and renewed. His oil reassures us that our God is not distant, nor does He leave us defenseless against the constant attacks on our minds and hearts. God draws us close, tending to our most vulnerable parts to secure us in who we are and who we belong to, the Good Shepherd. Where we are broken, He heals us. When we are restless, He provides peace. The anointing of the Holy Spirit sets us apart from the rest. "You anoint my head with oil" is a declaration of ownership and value by our Heavenly Father.

PART XI
Psalm 23

¹ The Lord is my shepherd, I lack nothing.

² He makes me lie down in green pastures, he leads me beside quiet waters,

³ he refreshes my soul. He guides me along the right paths for his name's sake.

⁴ Even though I walk through the darkest valley, I will fear no evil, for you are with me; your rod and your staff, they comfort me.

⁵ You prepare a table before me in the presence of my enemies. You anoint my head with oil; **my cup overflows.**

⁶ Surely your goodness and love will follow me all the days of my life, and I will dwell in the house of the Lord forever.

"my cup overflows.".

A cup or orange juice and a lifetime of favor

Memories of my kids that will constantly bring me joy, are when they are in the toddler phase, and they try to do basic activities they see the adults in their lives doing. This includes such activities as sweeping, vacuuming, or washing the dishes. They display a focused determination for success. A sheer will to accomplish an activity they have seen their mommy and daddy do. One memory that brings a smile to my face every time, is the first time my youngest daughter tried to pour her own glass of orange juice for the first time. My wife and I knew what the outcome would be, but she pleaded for the opportunity to try it herself.

She was sitting on my wife's lap at the kitchen table. In front of her sat a gallon of orange juice about three-quarters full, and a glass.

She asked my wife, *"Mommy, can I pour my glass of orange juice?"*. My wife's eyebrows rose in wonder as she looked at me for confirmation. I shrugged my shoulders, and she replied, *"sure honey"*, and my daughter smiled with surprise and excitement.

With both hands, my daughter grabs the juice jug and begins to tilt it. You can tell she's using every ounce of her strength to control it. At first, a few drops splash into the glass. Then a stream. Then a river.

"Okay, sweetie, it's getting to the top," my wife says gently. But the jug keeps tilting.

"All right, honey, it's almost full," she says again, this time with a touch of urgency.

My daughter doesn't flinch. The carton is almost completely upside down now.

"Sweetheart, it's full, it's full, it's full!"

By the time my wife reaches out to stop her, juice is spilling over the rim of the cup, running down the sides, spreading across the table. My wife's hands barely graze the jug before my daughter shouts with a voice full of defiance and pride, *"No, Mommy! I'm pouring the juice!"*

My wife pulls back her hands and lets her finish. The last few drops fall, and finally my daughter sets the empty carton down with a satisfied smile. Beaming with pride, and orange juice everywhere, *she* says *"See mommy, I did it."*

My wife just smiles, kisses her on the top of her head, and says, *"Good job, honey."*

It was such a small and beautiful moment. When I think of the words "my cup overflows," this is the scene that comes to mind. That is how I imagine God's heart toward us. His generosity is beyond measure. With a steady hand, he is unhurried, and unwilling to hold back. His blessings continuously spill over, not just filling some areas of our lives but overflowing beyond our expectations and onto the people around us. God's love, care, and favor seeping into our relationships, our work life, our joy, even our struggles.

When David wrote "my cup overflows," he wasn't just talking about abundance in things we can see. He was also describing the experience of being loved completely by the Good

Shepherd. A Good Shepherd who provides just what we need and more than we could ever contain. A cup of love and favor that keeps pouring, long after we think the glass is full.

my cup overflows...

In biblical times, an overflowing cup was symbolic of honor and welcome. At a banquet or gathering, when a host kept his guests' cups filled to overflowing, it was the hosts way of showing honor and appreciation in their presence. They wanted to ensure that their guests wanted for nothing. A cup was a symbol for provision. In this verse, David's imagery goes beyond providing a full cup, to an overflowing cup, which demonstrates abundance beyond need and earthly imaginations. David is pointing to a divine reality that in the Lord's presence, we are sustained, honored, welcomed, and freely given supernatural favor by God.

When David declares, "my cup overflows," he is referencing the genuine reality of a sheep in the constant care of the shepherd. The responsibility and duties of a shepherd were not merely on a "as needed" basis. Being a shepherd was a 24-hour, 7 days a week obligation. The shepherd was the provider, protector, and caretaker. They needed to be skilled agriculturist, veterinarian, and animal scientist. Every detail of a sheep's existence was in the hands of the shepherd. A good shepherd knew the terrain, where to find still water or dig wells, which pastures could sustain grazing and for how long, how to guide the flock safely through barren stretches of wilderness, how to patch up wounds and injuries, and how to keep them safe from lurking predators. For the sheep, survival was never a matter of their own skill or strength, it was entirely dependent on the shepherd's wisdom and provision, and in the care of a good shepherd the sheep's' cup overflows.

This analogy illustrates how God cares for us. Just as a sheep cannot secure their own water or refuge, we cannot sustain life apart from God's provision. Scripture reminds us that every good gift comes from the Lord. He not only provides what we need but does so in ways that go beyond sufficiency into abundance. Overflowing provision is constantly at work in our daily lives, both knowingly and unknowingly, seen and unseen.

James 1:17 17 Every good and perfect gift is from above, coming down from the Father of the heavenly lights, who does not change like shifting shadows.

Throughout the entire bible we read about the Lord intervening and interceding in the lives of His people:

- **Deuteronomy 31:6-8** 6 Be strong and courageous. Do not be afraid or terrified because of them, for the Lord your God goes with you; he will never leave you nor forsake you." 7 Then Moses summoned Joshua and said to him in the presence of all Israel, "Be strong and courageous, for you must go with this people into the land that the Lord swore to their ancestors to give them, and you must divide it among them as their inheritance. 8 The Lord himself goes before you and will be with you; he will never leave you nor forsake you. Do not be afraid; do not be discouraged."

- **Psalm 121:1-9** 1I lift up my eyes to the mountains, where does my help come from? 2 My help comes from the Lord, the Maker of heaven and earth. 3 He will not let your foot slip, he who watches over you will not slumber; 4 indeed, he who watches over Israel will neither slumber nor sleep. 5 The Lord watches over you, the Lord is your shade at

your right hand; 6 the sun will not harm you by day, nor
the moon by night. 7 The Lord will keep you from all harm,
he will watch over your life; 8 the Lord will watch over your
coming and going both now and forevermore.

- **Ephesians 3:16-21** 16 I pray that out of his glorious
  riches he may strengthen you with power through his
  Spirit in your inner being, 17 so that Christ may dwell in
  your hearts through faith. And I pray that you, being
  rooted and established in love, 18 may have power, together
  with all the Lord's holy people, to grasp how wide and long
  and high and deep is the love of Christ, 19 and to know this
  love that surpasses knowledge, that you may be filled to
  the measure of all the fullness of God. 20 Now to him who is
  able to do immeasurably more than all we ask or imagine,
  according to his power that is at work within us, 21 to him
  be glory in the church and in Christ Jesus throughout all
  generations, for ever and ever! Amen.

All the Lord's provisions have a purpose. Whether it be
physical provision food, water, shelter, and health, or spiritual
provisions of guidance, love, and protection; they are all
provided to direct us to His will for our lives, and His
provisions show up in varying circumstances. These
provisions manifest in opportunities that stretch us, times that
strengthen us, and circumstances that carry us when we
thought we could not go on. These blessings of provision,
sustain us when we feel like we are at a dead end, and because
of his grace, Hid provisions go far beyond anything that we
could ever imagine, earn, or deserve. Just like a cup that gets
filled past its brim, the Lord's provisions upon our lives are
not limited to one area, but overflow into every aspect of our

existence from our physical bodies, our minds, our emotions, and to spirit. As Paul wrote

2 Corinthians 9:8 [8] And God is able to bless you abundantly, so that in all things at all times, you have all that you need, you will abound in every good work".

Physical overflow

A shepherd's careful and diligent planning ensures that the flock's physical needs are met in every season. Food, water, ointments and oils, shade, and shelter are examples of the provision that are needs for the sheep's survival. A good shepherd will work tirelessly to make sure each, and every physical need of their sheep are met. In our lives. God does not just drop our physical needs of water, food and shelter in our laps. In all His majesty and glory, the Good Shepherd meets our physical needs while drawing us closer to Him and uplifting His Kingdom, all at the same time. The apostle Paul reminds us, "And my God will meet all your needs according to the riches of his glory in Christ Jesus" (**Philippians 4:19**). In the ancient world, a host that filled a cup to overflow proved that he was not stingy or cautious with his resources but lavish in his giving. The Good Shepherd fills our "cup" the same way. Not with "just enough" to scrape by but bountifully reflecting the essence of His generous and good nature towards us, his sheep.

Overflow through peace

In the wilderness, a shepherd would sometimes create secret pools of water. They dug pools carefully, clearing the debris, and shaping the brush so the water remained hidden and clean for the sheep. He would then direct his flock to these secret pools. This gave the sheep the sense of calmness and peace to drink without fear of attack. Likewise, God gives us peace that steadies us even when life feels uncertain and out of our control. Jesus promised,

John 14:27 27 Peace I leave with you; my peace I give you. I do not give to you as the world gives

He knows when our hearts, minds, and emotions become overwhelmed, anxious and fearful. Jesus desires to take us to His secret pools that gives us our sense of peace and rest for our souls. A peace that overflows into our hearts, into the depth of our emotions, and quiets the storms of fear, anxiety, and uncertainty.

Overflow through relationships

Sheep thrive in flocks. They feel safer, calmer, and healthier when they are joined together with other sheep. A good shepherd fosters that community, keeping the flock together fortifying each sheep from isolation and potential danger. In this same way, God blesses us with relationships that pour into our divine cups of life. Family, friends, colleagues, mentors, and a body of believers in Christ.

Ecclesiastes 4:9-12 tells us, 9 Two are better than one, because they have a good return for their labor: 10 If either of them falls down, one can help the other up. But pity anyone who falls and has no one to help them up. 11 Also, if two lie down together, they will keep warm. But how can one keep warm alone? 12 Though one may be overpowered, two can defend themselves. A cord of three strands is not quickly broken.

Not all relationships are godly cup fillers, some may be cup drainers or sadly cup destroyers. Yet even here, God works as the Good Shepherd. He teaches us to discern which relationships bring life and which pull us away from His will and what is best for us. Godly relationships allow us to grow and mature into the best versions of ourselves. The overflow comes when we nurture and walk with those who encourage and sharpen us in our faith to follow Jesus, who hold us accountable to the truth of God's word, and remind us of God's will, even when our own vision is clouded. Relationships rooted in love, and a shared faith become the evidence of God's overflow.

Overflow as witness

When our Good Shepherd fills our cup to the point of running over, it is not meant for us to collect the overflow and save it for later. That overflow should become our testimony and blessing to others. In ancient times, a brimming cup declared favor to all present. Similarly, when our cup is filled to overflow everyone around can see. But our God does not stop there. When God fills our cup, overflowing our lives with grace, peace, and provisions, it should spill into the lives of those around us.

Matthew 5:14-16 14 "You are the light of the world. A town built on a hill cannot be hidden. 15 Neither do people light a lamp and put it under a bowl. Instead, they put it on its stand, and it gives light to everyone in the house. 16 In the same way, let your light shine before others, that they may see your good deeds and glorify your Father in heaven.

Peter 4:9-11 9 Offer hospitality to one another without grumbling. 10 Each of you should use whatever gift you have received to serve others, as faithful stewards of God's grace in its various forms. 11 If anyone speaks, they should do so as one who speaks the very words of God. If anyone serves, they should do so with the strength God provides, so that in all things God may be praised through Jesus Christ. To him be the glory and the power for ever and ever. Amen.

Proverbs 11:25 25 A generous person will prosper; whoever refreshes others will be refreshed.

Summary

When David declares, "my cup overflows," he is not simply describing a fortunate season. He is testifying to the ongoing, daily reality of life with the Good Shepherd. The overflowing cup of Psalm 23 is not about material gain and excess but about an incredible divine abundance. Our Good Shepherd goes beyond providing for basic survival. He wants to fill our lives with peace, grace, relationships, and spiritual strength. Our cup should spill far beyond blessing our individual lives, but into the lives of those around us, bearing witness to the Lord's amazing grace, goodness, and glory.

David's proclamation, "my cup overflows" is not speaking of a life without hardship, but of a life grounded in the Shepherd's abundance. Sheep do not measure their well-being by how barren the wilderness appeared around them, but by the care and provision of their shepherd. In the same way, our overflowing cup does not depend on external circumstances, but on the presence of the One who provides all things.

"My cup overflows" is not a cleaver or catchy phrase, but it is a declaration of truth. It is a testimony of faith and trust in the Lord. David was not boasting of his own riches or glory but drawing attention to the Good Shepherd's love and care to fill, refill, and overflow our cups.

In this overflowing cup we see four truths:
1. It is the Good Shepherd's provision that sustains us in this life with more than enough.

2. It is the Good Shepherd's Spirit that fills us with peace, joy, and living water, that flourishes our lives

3. It is the Good Shepherd's love that turns our personal blessing into a public witness of His goodness.

4. It is the Good Shepherd's generosity that allows us to be a blessing to others through the amazing blessings He has provides.

PART XII
Psalm 23

¹ The Lord is my shepherd, I lack nothing.

² He makes me lie down in green pastures, he leads me beside quiet waters,

³ he refreshes my soul. He guides me along the right paths for his name's sake.

⁴ Even though I walk through the darkest valley, I will fear no evil, for you are with me; your rod and your staff, they comfort me.

⁵ You prepare a table before me in the presence of my enemies. You anoint my head with oil; my cup overflows.

⁶ **Surely your goodness and love will follow me all the days of my life,** and I will dwell in the house of the Lord forever.

"Surely your goodness and love will follow me all the days of my life"

Hazard Lights and Hard Lessons

Growing up, I rode the bus to school. Yes, exactly what you're picturing, yellow, loud, and clunky, with endless rows of brown vinyl seats that stuck to your legs in the summer and felt like ice blocks in the winter. There was no heat, and no air conditioning, just the steady rumble of the engine and the smell of diesel mixed with peanut butter sandwiches.

Every school I attended was about two miles from my home, a quick five-minute car ride, but a solid twenty-minute bus commute with all the neighborhood stops. From the beginning, my parents made it very clear to my brother and me that the school bus, provided by the district, was our ride to school. In the rain rain, snow, sleet, or sunshine, we would be on that bus until we could drive ourselves to school. Our parents refused to shuffle us to or from school. So, each day we endured a ride on the yellow steel giant.

Anyone who rode the school bus to school knew that you had to be up and ready, the bus was waiting for no one. That rule didn't bother me when I was young. I was one of those kids who popped out of bed before sunrise, full of energy and ready to go. But by sixth grade, things changed. Sleep started to become a necessity. The idea of waking up early to stand out in the cold no longer carried any joy.

There is one particular school morning that stands out greater than all the rest. It was late November in Colorado and the kind of morning where the air bit your face and frost painted every windowpane. My Looney Tunes alarm clock went off prompting at 6:30 am, sounding the alarm and vibrating my nightstand. I smacked it silent and rolled right back over. Sometime later, I felt a hand on my arm.

"T, get up. You're running late, let's get moving" my mom said, her voice firm but calm.

 I grumbled, rubbed my eyes, and sat up. Everything that morning felt slower, washing my face, brushing my teeth, putting on each piece of clothing was in slow motion. I figured I had plenty of time to get ready and get to the bus stop. The school bus was never on schedule and odds were high that it would be late. Besides, it was freezing outside. Why should I rush to stand in the cold I thought.

After I ate breakfast, I grabbed my backpack, kissed my mom goodbye, and headed out the door. The bus stop was just around the corner and usually, by the time I got there, a few kids would be waiting. This morning, the corner was empty. Not a single soul waiting. I tilted my head in curiosity, looked down the street, and no bus in sight. I waited five minutes, then ten until it dawned on me, I had missed the bus. I knew I needed to head back home and tell my mom that I missed the bus. Instead of returning swiftly, I drug me feet, my backpack felt heavier, and I could already picture my mom's face when I told her that I had missed the bus. I walked in through the garage, into the house, and found her in her room.

"Mom... I missed the bus."

She turned, eyebrows raised. *"What?"*

"I missed it. Sorry." I replied

Her sigh said it all. She didn't yell, just gave a small shake of her head, walked into her closet, and came out a few minutes later dressed and ready to go. *"Let's go,"* she said. I followed her into the garage, slid into the passenger seat, and started to close the door when she looked over at me.

"What are you doing?" she said.

"Getting in the car." I replied, with a look of confusion plastered across my face.

With no hesitating she shots back, *"I told you, if you miss the bus, I'm not driving you to school."*

I blinked, with more confusion *"So, what am I supposed to do?"*

She folded her arms. *"I don't believe your legs are broken. You'd better start walking. And you'd better hurry because if you're late to class, you will be in even more trouble."*

"Wait, what? You're making me walk?" I asked with shock and disappointment.

It was clear, my parent's rule of not driving us to school was going to stand. I got out the car and started walking. I was still stunned in disbelief. As I left the neighborhood, I looked back, and there she was, creeping along behind me in her car. The hazard lights were flashing, and I supposed the car was barely going three miles an hour. As we hit the main busy road, embarrassment began to sink in. Cars were honking and swerving around her, some drivers glaring as they passed. Was this really happening, I thought.

I continued my walk to school, the fridged chill in the winter air was no comparison to the humiliation I felt. I tried cutting through a side neighborhood to escape the main road, but her car rolled up beside me again. With that, she rolled down the window.

"Boy, stop playing and keep going," she said, her voice half stern, and half amused.

So, I kept walking. For those two and a half miles, my mom never left my side, her headlights on me the entire way like a stage spotlight. By the time we reached the school, I was sweaty, my face was flush, and I was thoroughly humiliated and humbled. She gave a quick honk, waved, and called out, *"Love you, honey! Have a great day!"* before driving off.

The entire day at school all I could think of was how my mom made me walk to school. That afternoon, when I got home, I couldn't hold it in. *"Mom,"* I said, *"if you were going to drive next to me the whole way, why couldn't I just ride with you?"*

She smiled, calm as ever. *"Well, "T "because your dad and I told you if you missed the bus, we wouldn't be your chauffer. So, it was time for you to learn a lesson. Yet at the same time,"* she paused for effect, *"I wasn't going to let anything happen to you. Just like this morning, I'll always be there, watching over you and keeping you safe."*

I didn't have the words for it then and at the time I couldn't understand. Now that I have kids of my own, I understand exactly what she was doing. She was teaching me a lesson in responsibility but also showing me presence. Often times a shepherd will follow behind their flock, letting them walk their path while keeping a protective watch. My mom was mirroring this tactic, letting me learn a valuable lesson while at the same time staying close enough to cover me if I stumbled. That day, I learned two things: The most practically don't miss the bus, especially in the winter. But the even greater lesson, even when it feels like you're walking alone, care and protections will allow no matter where I go.

"Surely your goodness and love will follow me"

This concluding verse of Psalm 23 is not merely an optimistic hope for the future. This final verse is an assertive proclamation, a confident declaration, a blessed assurance in the unchanging, unwavering, steadfast faithfulness of God. David begins this final verse by reflecting upon all that his Good Shepherd has already done for him in verses 1-5:

- **Declaration of ownership** – "The Lord is my shepherd"
- **Providing for all needs** - "I lack nothing"
- **Remover of fear and worry** – "He makes me lie down in green pastures"
- **Guide to the essential of life** – "he leads me beside quite waters"
- **Restorer and rejuvenator of our innermost being** – "he refreshes my soul"
- **Setting the course for a prosperous life** – "He guides me along the right paths for his name's sake"
- **Bestowing nearness and companionship through the toughest journeys of life** – "Even though I walk

through the darkest valley, I will fear no evil, for you are with me

- **Giver of Protection and authority combined with guidance and care** – "your rod and your staff, they comfort me"
- **Architect of our provision and protection** – "You prepare a table before me in the presence of my enemies"
- **Safeguarding against mental attacks of the enemy** – "You anoint my head with oil"
- **Provider of abundance beyond needs and wants** – "my cup overflows"

From the Good Shepherd's guidance and provisions to His protection and companionship and everything in-between, David's reflection establishes that the Good Shepherd is our guarantee and assurance in life. This well-established guarantee gave David great faith, and now it gives us the ability to not live in fear of what we face presently or in the future. We can live with sure confidence that it is not about what we go through in life, but who is with us, our Good Shepherd. The Good Shepherd has safeguarded, restored, and set our course will continue to do so as we follow Him.

Close your eyes with me and visualize God's goodness and love following you through your life. What are you seeing? A beautiful scene of yourself smiling ear to ear skipping though a meadow with God's love and mercy shining behind you? Or perhaps you picture a herd of beautiful gazelle being chased by an oncoming lion? Whatever visual you create, God should be there with you, pursuing you always. The original Hebrew word "follow" utilized in this verse is "radaph." Radaph is means *to pursue, to chase after, or hunt*. This Hebrew word carries an intensity connected to its meaning. Radaph alludes

to a passionate and vigorous pursuit, telling us that God's
goodness and persistent love are not just lagging behind us
passively. His goodness and love are chasing us down to
overtake us with his mercy, provision, and grace, **"all the
days of my life."**

Lamentations 3:22–23 22 Because of the Lord's great
love we are not consumed, for his compassions never fail.
23 They are new every morning; great is your faithfulness.

Deuteronomy 31:6 6 Be strong and courageous. Do not be
afraid or terrified because of them, for the Lord your God goes
with you; he will never leave you nor forsake you."

John 14:15-20 15 "If you love me, keep my commands. 16 And
I will ask the Father, and he will give you another advocate to
help you and be with you forever, 17 the Spirit of truth. The
world cannot accept him, because it neither sees him nor
knows him. But you know him, for he lives with you and will
be in you. 18 I will not leave you as orphans; I will come to
you. 19 Before long, the world will not see me anymore, but you
will see me. Because I live, you also will live. 20 On that
day you will realize that I am in my Father, and you are in me,
and I am in you.

When we think of how our Good Shepherd passionately
chases after us, it reshapes how we can understand our past,
our present and our future. Every past success, win, rescue,
and save is a testimony of God's providential presence in our
lives. His diligent hands paved the road for our blessings.
Every day, we can look to our present circumstances and know
that the Good Shepherd will provide the provisions for our

success, day by day. In regard to our future, through grace by faith in who follows us, we can take hold of the words in **Romans 8:28** [28] And we know that in all things God works for the good of those who love him, who have been called according to his purpose.

Summary

Sheep are oblivious of what is happening around them, they graze, eat, rest, sleep, and follow the guidance of their shepherd blindly. Sheep are never concerned with the shepherd's staff guarding them from predators. They are clueless of the path that has been meticulously set, and naïve to the pasture that has been tended for their prosperity. Nevertheless, sheep live safely because of the shepherd's constant attention. Likewise, we often go through life unaware of the trials and valleys that lie ahead, but we can always keep the insurance that our Good Shepherd who was, is, and will forever be, is the overseer in our lives. Dangers we did not see are removed, doors we did not unlock are opened, and even doors we thought we wanted to walk through are closed and locked for our well-being. We once were aimless as sheep wondering though this life, but the Good Shepherd has curated a life for us with purpose and meaning.

Psalms 32:8 [8] I will instruct you and teach you in the way you should go; I will counsel you with my loving eye on you. When we grasp this truth, gratitude begins to overflow.

We stop measuring God's faithfulness only by what we can see in front of us and start trusting in what has been carefully constructed and actively designed for us all along. Therefore, when we reflect on the landscape of our lives, the lush pastures, the on looking predators, the caverns and valleys, the cool crisp streams, and the mountain tops, like David, we can confidently and assertively proclaim our God's goodness and love have been, currently are, and forever will follows us.

Romans 8:37–39 37 No, in all these things we are more than conquerors through him who loved us. 38 For I am convinced that neither death nor life, neither angels nor demons, neither the present nor the future, nor any powers, 39 neither height nor depth, nor anything else in all creation, will be able to separate us from the love of God that is in Christ Jesus our Lord.

Psalm 139:1-18 1 You have searched me, Lord, and you know me. 2 You know when I sit and when I rise; you perceive my thoughts from afar. 3 You discern my going out and my lying down; you are familiar with all my ways. 4 Before a word is on my tongue you, Lord, know it completely. 5 You hem me in behind and before, and you lay your hand upon me. 6 Such knowledge is too wonderful for me, too lofty for me to attain. 7 Where can I go from your Spirit? Where can I flee from your presence? 8 If I go up to the heavens, you are there; if I make my bed in the depths, you are there. 9 If I rise on the wings of the dawn, if I settle on the far side of the sea, 10 even there your hand will guide me, your right hand will hold me fast. 11 If I say, "Surely the darkness will hide me and the light become night around me," 12 even the darkness will not be dark to you; the night will shine like the day, for darkness is as light to you. 13 For you created my inmost being you knit me together in my mother's womb. 14 I praise you because I am fearfully and wonderfully made; your works are wonderful; I know that full well. 15 My frame was not hidden from you when I was made in the secret place, when I was woven together in the

depths of the earth. ¹⁶ Your eyes saw my unformed body; all
the days ordained for me were written in your book before one
of them came to be. ¹⁷ How precious to me are your thoughts,
God! How vast is the sum of them! ¹⁸ Were I to count them,
they would outnumber the grains of sand, when I awake, I am
still with you.

PART XIII
Psalm 23

¹ The Lord is my shepherd, I lack nothing.

² He makes me lie down in green pastures, he leads me beside quiet waters,

³ he refreshes my soul. He guides me along the right paths for his name's sake.

⁴ Even though I walk through the darkest valley, I will fear no evil, for you are with me; your rod and your staff, they comfort me.

⁵ You prepare a table before me in the presence of my enemies. You anoint my head with oil; my cup overflows.

⁶ Surely your goodness and love will follow me all the days of my life, **and I will dwell in the house of the Lord forever**.

"and I will dwell in the house of the Lord forever."

"I don't understand, but okay"

Have you ever had one of those moments when your young child, any child for that matter, changes your whole perspective on life? This is a regular occurrence for me. My children are constantly challenging my perceptions on life. There is one time in particular that is stamped in my mind. It was one of those crisp Denver mornings when the air felt light but carried just enough chill to make you zip your coat up. My wife and I parked several blocks from an event in downtown Denver, and our daughter, who was about four at the time, walked between us, her tiny hands holding each of ours swinging without a care in the world. The city was alive that morning, cars racing by the scent of roasted coffee drifting out from corner cafés, and the rhythmic sound of footsteps echoing along the sidewalk. That morning, my daughter was curious about everything as most four-year-olds are. As we walked the streets, she was taking it all in; the tall buildings, the flashing lights of crosswalks, and the street performers that seemed to appear on every block.

Then, suddenly, she slowed her pace and tugged at my hand. *"Daddy, why is that man sleeping outside?"*

I followed her gaze and saw a man lying on a thin blanket against the cold concrete, his belongings packed into a grocery cart beside him. For a moment, I was silent, searching for words that a four-year-old could understand.

"I'm not sure, honey," I said finally. *"Not everyone has a home or a place to go sleep inside like we do."*

Her brow furrowed, and I could almost hear the next question forming before she said it, *"well, why not, Daddy?"*

That one question turned into ten more questions. Why didn't he have money? Why couldn't he stay with his family? Why didn't someone build a big hotel for everyone who didn't have a home? Her little voice was steady, innocent, and full of genuine concern. I tried my best to answer her; however, each response was followed by another gentle "why," until I found myself saying words I didn't expect to say to a preschooler.

"Well, honey, there are a lot of economics involved in that answer."

She tilted her head. *"What's eco-MOM-ics, Daddy?"*

I couldn't help but laugh. *"It's eco-NOM-ics, baby,"* I responded.

"What does that mean?" she replied.

That was the moment I realized I was in too deep and out of my expertise. I pulled out my phone, and told her *"let's look it up together."* Google to the rescue. I inputted a simple search, why do some people not have housing? The search results yielded a combination of results including, affordable housing, stagnating income, social safety nets, and economic downturns. I read her a variety of the different answers the search provided. When I finished, she was quiet for a moment.

"So, are people trying to fix this, Daddy?"

"Yes, honey. There are people trying every day to help."

She nodded, then said something I didn't expect. *"Okay."*

I looked down at her, puzzled. *"Okay? You don't understand, though."*

She smiled and shrugged in that sweet, matter-of-fact way only a child can. *"No, I don't, but I trust you, Daddy. You said people are helping, so I trust you."*

That moment hit me harder than most keynote speeches I'd heard. The way she said it, calm, certain, with no doubt in her voice, stopped me in my tracks. My daughter didn't need all the answers and didn't need to understand every detail. It was enough that her father said, "I've got it." That was all she needed to rest easy.

Wouldn't it be something if we could trust God like that? To hold His hand through the uncertainties of this world and simply say, "I don't understand, but I trust You?" God, unlike me, truly does know everything. He sees the full picture when all we can see are small snapshots that don't seem to fit together. Just as my daughter found comfort in trusting her father's limited wisdom, we too have the opportunity to find everlasting fellowship and peace in our Heavenly Father.

The walk of life takes us through busy streets, cold winds, and scenes we can't always make sense of. When we choose to rest in the Good Shepherd's presence and trust His care, we find the assurance David declared in the final verse of the psalm:

"And I will dwell in the house of the Lord forever." To dwell in His house means to live in the safety and assurance that is found in the presence and love of God. When we dwell in the Good Shepherd's house, we can find rest regardless of what we don't understand, or what we are going through because there is One who possess the full picture from the beginning to the end. We can choose to always walk hand in hand with our Good Shepherd. Knowing He loves and cares for us more than we can ever ask or imagine.

"And I will dwell in the house of the Lord forever"

For sheep, the dwelling created by the shepherd means everything. Their safety, nourishment, protection, peace, and overall well-being are all tied to the shepherd's diligence and care. Their entire existence is connected to the shepherd. Every decision a shepherd makes is about the well-being of the flock.

As David guides us through this Psalm, he transitions the Good Shepherd's care from "the valley of the shadow of death," which depicts fear, and life's dangers, to concluding this Psalm with the assurance that this care is not temporary, but eternal. As David thoughtfully crafted the closing words of Psalm 23, he was deliberate in communicating these words as more than an eloquent conclusion but as an everlasting decree of eternal belonging, and an unbroken fellowship with the greatest shepherd of all.

I will dwell

To "dwell" with the shepherd means to live under the constant oversight and protection, and within proximity and presence. Away from the shepherd's care for the slightest amount of time, leaves the sheep vulnerable and susceptible to danger. David's time as a shepherd before he was king, gave him insight to write in figurative language that describes heavenly realities through the lens of the sheep and the lens of the Shepherd. When David said, "I will dwell," it wasn't a hesitant assertion, it was a confident expectation. David's trust in the Lord, as his Good Shepherd, gave him the confidence that the Lord's care on his life was far greater than anything he could do on his own.

To dwell spiritually with our Lord, means to draw close to Him in obedience. That dwelling gives us the ability trust in His guidance through humility, to believe in his promises through faith, and to receive the eternal hope by faith. The statement "I will dwell" was about complete submission to the will and the way of the Lord over David's life. David continued to express this longing in Psalms 27:1-4

Psalms 27:1-4 1 The Lord is my light and my salvation, whom shall I fear? The Lord is the stronghold of my life, of whom shall I be afraid? 2 When the wicked advance against me to devour me, it is my enemies and my foes who will stumble and fall. 3 Though an army besiege me, my heart will not fear; though war break out against me, even then I will be confident. 4 One thing I ask from the Lord, this only do I seek: that I may dwell in the house of the Lord all the days of my life, to gaze on the beauty of the Lord and to seek him in his temple."

The same can be true of our relationship with God. We too have the opportunity to dwell in the heavenly reality of His house and allow Him to be our Good Shepherd all the days of our life. We have been given the ability to abide under the

Good Shepherd's care, guidance, protection and love. Through Jesus' death and resurrection, The Good Shepherd opened the door to an eternal dwelling with him. Through Jesus Christ, this opportunity to dwell has been made available to every believer. To "dwell in the house of the Lord" is to live daily with an assurance of nearness and trust in the Lord. It means acknowledging His presence on our jobs, with our families, in every decision we make, and even in every word we speak. It means allowing His Holy Spirit to govern our thoughts, His Word to guide our paths, and His presence to comfort and correct us.

Forever

A good shepherd doesn't simply tend to the immediate needs of their flock. They must also be focused ahead to tomorrow, the next season, the next voyage, the next pasture. They know their sheep need more than daily provision; they also need lasting security and care. To dwell in the house of the Lord forever, is to be aware of the continuous presence and protection of the Good Shepherd. Jesus affirms this truth when he stated to His disciples in **John 14:2** "2 My Father's house has many rooms; if that were not so, would I have told you that I am going there to prepare a place for you?". He assured them that the Shepherd who guides them in life is also the one preparing their eternal dwelling place. Our dwelling with Him can begin here on this Earth, as His Holy Spirit lives within us. But it does not stop there.

This closing verse of Psalm 23 is not just a prolific ending to the story of a beautiful journey through life under a shepherd's care. This ending is the foreshadowing of His eternal plan. It is the culmination of a voyage that begins with fellowship and ends with eternal companionship. In the end, Psalm 23 is the story of a relationship. A relationship that originates in trust, is sustained by care, and ends in eternal communion. The story of a Good Shepherd who leads us beside still waters and restores our souls and prepares a home for us in His presence forever. His goodness and mercy pursue us not only through the days of this life but into eternity itself. We, like David, can rest in the confident assurance: **"I will dwell in the house of the Lord forever."**

Summary

David's assertion, "I will dwell in the house of the Lord forever," is not a quiet wish but a bold and confident statement of faith. This verse reflects the heart of someone who has learned through every season, pasture, valley, enemy, and overflowing cup, that the Good Shepherd's care is sufficient and never-ending. This final line completes the journey of Psalm 23, showing us that God's goodness does not stop when the path grows dark or uncertain. The same Shepherd who leads, restores, and protects, also welcomes us into His eternal home. His care stretches beyond the boundaries of time; what He begins in our lives here, He continues in our eternal home together with him.

Ultimately, this verse reminds us that the Good Shepherd's goal is and has always been relationship. The plan of God was not yet unveiled within the Scriptures of the Old Testament, but David poetic language foreshadowed the greatest gift to come, "the Lord is my shepherd, I lack nothing." He leads us, not just to green pastures or quiet waters, but back to Him. Every act of the Good Shepherd's care points toward His plan and his will to bring us into His kingdom. It is there and there alone that we can find true belonging, purpose, and peace. The Good Shepherd who began the journey with us in verse one will be the same one who welcomes us home in the New Heaven and the New Earth (Rev.21-22), and we will dwell in His House with him FOREVER.

Closing Prayer

Lord, you are our Good Shepherd, and I thank you that your care does not end when the day is over or the journey grows long. You lead us through seasons of joy and sorrow, through valleys and over mountaintops. You never once leave our side. Teach us to live with a constant awareness of your presence. May our hearts be your dwelling place, where your peace rests and the Holy Spirit reigns. Thank you that you chose us, through grace by faith, to dwell in your house today, and forevermore.

Father, help us to remember that your goodness and mercy are not distant promises but daily realities. Also remind us that you are pursuing us in every moment. When we grow weary, remind us that you have gone before us to prepare a place where we will dwell with you forever. Let hope anchor our souls and steady our faith.

Good Shepherd of our lives, thank you for calling us yours. May our lives reflect our trust in you, the one who guides us through the Holy Spirit to our heavenly home. Until that day when faith becomes sight, we will follow you, rest in you, and dwell in your love, now and forever.

In Jesus' name
Amen.

Acknowledgments

Writing this book has reminded me that no single person is an island, and certainly, no Christian walks alone. While it is my name on the cover, the wisdom within these pages is a mosaic of the voices, prayers, and knowledge of my community, and I am deeply honored and humbled to belong to it.

To My Spiritual Mentors and Guides

I want to thank the teachers and pastors who didn't just teach me the Word but showed me how to live it. From sermons and bibles studies, your spiritual guidance has set the foundation for my life. Especially to those who sat across from me in coffee shops, zooms calls, church pews or shot baskets with me in empty gyms. Thank you for your discernment and always pointing me back to the Cross.

To My Inner Circle

To my family, thank you for always allowing me to be my true authentic self, without shame or judgement. You have anyways had unwavering belief in my hopes and dreams. Your grace and encouragement during my moments of doubt are the tangible hands and feet of Jesus for me each and every day.

To the "Quiet" Encouragers

There are those of you who sent a timely text, offered a prayer when you didn't know I was struggling, or provided a meal when life felt heavy. You may think your contribution was small, but in God's economy, nothing is wasted. You are needed fuel in my journey.

To the Reader
Thank you for holding these words. My prayer is that you find the same comfort and challenge that my community has so graciously given to me all the years of my life.

My Wife
While many people planted seeds, you are the one who tended the soil every single day. You are my greatest earthly blessing, my most constant prayer, and the clearest evidence I have a Good Shepherd. I spent months trying to put the character of Christ into sentences, only to realize I was simply describing what I see in you. This book was birthed in the space your love created for me. Thank you for loving me with a patience that humbles me and a passion that inspires me.